IN HIS PRESENCE

A DEVOTIONAL JOURNEY
TO EXPERIENCE
GOD'S PRESENCE

JOTHAN WHITE

Scriptures are from The King James Version of the Bible, *The Thompson-Chain Reference Bible Fifth Improved Edition,* B.B. Kirkbride Bible Co., Inc.

ISBN: 978-1-7372568-0-9 (paperback)

FOREWORD

These devotions were written to help us know who we are in Christ and how to truly feel the presence of God. They confirm how we can be conformed and established in the Word of God. Dr. White wants us to know that there is a struggle with the flesh, mind, and spirit as God has given us in His Word, but through studying and meditating on His Word daily we will learn how to overcome the struggles.

The book helps us to take a good look at self and to see ourselves as God created us. It helps us to understand that as children of God we are heirs of God and have many benefits which he has established for us. Dr. White shares this information in these devotional readings.

The devotions are designed to help us know who we are and how to conform our minds to both God's Word and the knowledge of God's presence in our lives at all times. These devotions also share with us how we can live our lives as God has ordained us.

I personally feel that from these devotions there can be an emerge-creative reconstruction of possible emotions and issues which can motivate men and women in establishing a true relationship with God.

This book allows us to take a closer look at who we are as believers in Christ and the affirmers of God's presence. I recommend as you read and meditate on these devotions that you allow the Holy Spirit to speak to you through your mind as God speaks through His Word.

Melvia D. Russell, Ph.D.
Christian Counselor

INTRODUCTION

The Bible teaches us that every good and perfect gift comes from God. (James 1:17) Even though we don't deserve anything from God, He, according to His everlasting mercy, gives us good gifts. He also gives us gifts that are not only good but are also perfect for us. He never gives us a gift that is not conducive to us. God is the source of everything good and perfect.

As it relates to God's gift to us, I am convinced that God's greatest gift to us has nothing to do with material things. Material things come and go. They have no lasting value. There is one thing God gives to those who are called by His name—the gift of His presence. He has promised, "I am with you always, even unto the end of the world. (Matthew 28:20b)

Can you imagine how miserable and hopeless life would be without the precious gift of God's presence? It is when we recognize and acknowledge God's presence that life begins to make sense. God has come along beside you to talk with you, to walk with you, and to empower you to do His will.

This book aims to enable the reader to become more conscious of God's presence in his/her life, to embrace God's presence, to engage in kingdom work according to God's plan for his/her life, and to help others along the way. In that light, the Apostle Paul charges us, "Therefore, my beloved brethren, be ye stedfast, unmoveable, always abounding in the work of the Lord, forasmuch as ye know that your labour is not in vain in the Lord." (1 Corinthians 15:58)

1

"Then there arose a reasoning among them, which of them should be greatest." (Luke 9:46)

It is challenging to go through life without arguing. People have been quarreling since the beginning of time, and they will continue to do so. Men and women engage in disputes for many reasons. The main reason is due to a difference in opinions. The truth is that most individuals tend to think they are right; therefore, they try to prove it by debating.

In a sense, disagreements can be helpful, especially when they are done in the right spirit and with the right motive. Through heated discussions, humankind can come to see the light and embrace new insights that will benefit their lives and the lives of others. Yes, there are times when a war of words is necessary and beneficial. The Bible is right: There is a time for everything under the heaven. (Ecclesiastes 3:1) Proving a point at the right time could save one's life. Do not be afraid to engage in a formal discussion of opposing points of view when there is a great need to do so for the glory of God and for the edifying of others.

On the other hand, some arguments are not very beneficial at all, since they are grounded in immature spiritual motives which produce selfish ambitions. Such was the case with the disciples of our Lord. Jesus had just cast a demon out of a young boy, an act which displayed the mighty power of God. It was in that setting that He told them about His death.

The disciples did not understand what Jesus was talking about. They were also afraid to ask Him to explain it to them. People do some strange things when they are scared. It was fear that led them to shift their focus from that which was paramount to that of little significance (i.e., who would be the greatest among them). What a waste of time. They put themselves before the mission. They lost sight of the divine agenda. Instead of seeking a place of service, they were seeking the most magnificent position.

Those men that Jesus, our Lord and Savior, had personally chosen for kingdom work had made themselves more important than the work. When we become more important than the vocation God called us to, we lose that heavenly perspective and embrace a worldly point of view. Then we start bickering about trivial things that have nothing to do with the kingdom of God and His righteousness. It is at this juncture that God's agenda begins to suffer and becomes less effective.

Jesus knew what the disciples were reasoning about. He used that opportunity to teach them about true greatness. He taught them to become childlike in their attitude and that greatness is about serving. "For he that is least among you all, the same shall be great." (Luke 9:48b) True greatness is about serving others and walking daily with Jesus.

What is our Lord saying to you right now about service? He is trying to get your attention. Are you paying Him any attention? He is speaking, but are you listening?

2

*"Search me, O God, and know my heart: try me, and know my thoughts: And see if **there be any** wicked way in me, and lead me in the way everlasting." (Psalm 139:23–24)*

We pray about many things. We make devout petitions to God regarding the well-being of our loved ones, community, church, and the world. We also commune with our Lord about implementing His will in our lives, in the lives of our loved ones, and in the world. We ask for guidance and for spiritual and physical healing. We also thank God for His goodness and many blessings showered upon us. These are just some of the things we talk about as we go to our Maker and Creator on bended knees. The list is endless.

We make supplications about the things that we are concerned about. Sometimes our requests are about our personal needs. Sometimes they are about the needs of others. Now and then, our invocations are selfish. At times they are God-centered. Regardless, it is a good thing to have a prayer life. Such a life indicates that we know we are insufficient in every way but are leaning and depending on God who is all-sufficient.

As we think about our prayer life, I wonder how often we call upon our Master about our loyalty to Him. Perhaps we don't do much soliciting or thinking in that area because we take it for granted. It is at this juncture that we need to learn from David, who did not take his loyalty to God for granted. He was serious about his faithfulness to his Creator. He had taken a good look at his relationship with God and was satisfied. He considered himself to be trustworthy to Yahweh. David also knew that we humans often think more highly of ourselves than we should. We often see the person we want to be rather than the person we are.

To avoid this mistake, David looked to the Lord God. He asked Yahweh to put His searchlight on him: to examine him thoroughly; to search his heart and thoughts to see if there were any sins that were conducive to disloyalty and make them known to him. Then David would confess his sins and receive the Divine's forgiveness. David believed God would lead him in the way of everlasting and would preserve his life.

Notice that David did not look to others who were less loyal than he was to confirm his loyalty to God. He did not ask his close companions about his commitment to the Almighty. He did not ask the priest or the prophet to examine his devotion to the Omnipotent. He went to God. Only God knew the complete truth about him.

Only God knows our hearts and thoughts completely. Let us go to Him, to His Word, to see any sin in us that is conducive to disloyalty so that we can confess our sins, find forgiveness, and be led in the way of everlasting. Thank God for His honesty and guidance. Do you look to God through His Word to reveal the truth about yourself? If not, why not?

3

"Now the God of hope fill you with all joy and peace in believing,
that ye may abound in hope, through the power of the Holy Ghost."
(Romans 15:13)

We are living in a world that is permeated with trouble, confusion, and disappointment. There seems to be a continual flow of dreadful news each day. People are perpetually endeavoring to escape the appalling predicament we are trapped in by using drugs and alcohol, which has proven to be unsuccessful. Some take vacations to forget about the troubles of this world, at least for a few moments; however, they must come back to reality. Some become overwhelmed by the troubles of this world and decide that the only solution is suicide.

There must be a real and vital answer to this problem. The answer cannot be found in human intellect. Our intelligence has failed us from the beginning of time in this regard. Do not misunderstand me; I am not suggesting that social astuteness is of no value. Personal wisdom has its advantages and has brought about much good. Yet while that may be, we must look beyond individual acumen to discover meaning and purpose. Meaning and purpose cannot exist without hope, joy, and peace.

Where do we find hope, joy, and peace in such a troubled world? The truth is that we must look beyond this world because such attributes do not belong to this world. The good news is that they are available to us. They are within our reach. We can enjoy and embrace hope, joy, and peace in this world that seems to have nothing to offer us but bad news. The answer is found in God and only in God. We must look to Him. We must put our trust in Him.

When hope appears to elude us, we must look to the God of hope because He always keeps His Word. He has given us His Word that He always has our best interest at heart, so much that He always works things out for our good. That being the case, we can always be hopeful because God has a plan that includes us. The good news about His plan is that He is capable of working it out, and He is working it out. Most of all, we are hopeful for the reason that our God is a God of hope.

As we put our trust in the God of hope, He gives us hope, joy, and peace through the Holy Spirit, even amid lousy news. The bad news of this world does not overwhelm us or cause us to succumb to despair and do something foolish. We can continuously think about and experience God's hope, joy, and peace that He gives us through the Holy Spirit. Are you experiencing this hope, joy, and peace because of your trust in God?

4

*"So Abram departed, as the LORD had spoken unto him; and Lot went with him: and Abram **was** seventy and five years old when he departed out of Haran." (Genesis 12:4)*

Many voices are speaking to us today. There is the voice of the world, our loved ones, our friends, and our flesh. Each of these expressions speaks to us loudly and clearly trying to influence us to take a specific direction in life. At times they are difficult to ignore and are very tempting, offering those things that are satisfying and pleasing to the flesh. Following any of these utterances will ultimately lead to disappointment and sorrow.

There is also another voice speaking, trying to get our attention. It is this speech that we need to listen to and follow. Even though this voice is also loud and clear, we sometimes fail to pay attention to it because it is not as inviting and tempting as the others are. It challenges us to follow a different path. It calls us to march to the beat of a different drummer. Frequently, this articulation challenges us to separate ourselves from people, places, and things that are so familiar to us. Obeying this voice takes more than a notion. It takes faith and courage. It is the ultimate utterance—the VOICE among many voices. It is the one that we should follow.

When Abraham heard this voice, he took the time to listen even though it was a voice that he was not familiar with. It was very distinct, authoritative, inspiring, and clear. It was God calling him to take a different path—a path that would separate him from everything he was familiar with and loved. It was the call of God for Abraham to embrace His plan (God's plan) and walk in it as if it were Abraham's very own plan. To do so, Abraham must turn his back to those things that were recognizable to him and embrace a future that he did not plan nor know anything about. Abraham was obedient. "So Abram departed, as the LORD had spoken unto him." (Genesis 12:4a)

God is still speaking today. He speaks in various ways. He speaks through our conscience. He converses through events and circumstances—good and bad. He talks through other people. Now and then, He articulates through His "still small voice." Most of all, He articulates through His Word. Are you willing to take the time to listen to God? He is speaking to you in one of these voices. Are you listening? He is calling you to be different from the world. Are you listening? He is calling you to a particular vocation. Are you paying attention? He is calling you to have a closer walk with Him. Are you taking notes? He is calling you to separate from those who mean you no good. Are you hearing Him? He is calling you to repent, turn from your wicked ways, turn to Him, and be saved. Are you ready to take action? Like Abraham, will you be obedient?

Being obedient to the call of God upon your life will not only bring blessings in your life but in the lives of those who are close to you. It will also bring blessings to strangers you meet along the way, since the way you live and your devotion to God will influence their lives. Obeying God will pay off in this life and in the life to come. That is a fact.

5

"Wherefore I say unto thee, her sins, which are many, are forgiven; for she loved much: but to whom little is forgiven, the same loveth little." (Luke 7:47)

Our Lord performed many great and unforgettable miracles when He walked among us. People were drawn to Him because of His ability to perform wonders. Jesus is still performing miracle today. The sick are being healed. He is still making a way out of no way. He has even brought to life those who have been pronounced clinically dead. There is no doubt; Jesus is still working supernatural happenings today. Just like the days of old, people are yet following Jesus because of what they can get from Him. They are fascinated by what Jesus can do for them.

I have surmised that the greatest miracle Jesus has performed and is still performing is the miracle of forgiveness. The truth is that we are all sinners. Some are religious sinners who claim to be righteous. Others are church-going sinners who hide behind the church as if going to church gains them points with God. Others are straight out sinners who feel no need for absolution. No matter what type of sinner we are we all need pardon. Without God's absolution, we are all condemned to death. If God refuses to remove our guilt, living is in vain, regardless of our accomplishments. It is a tremendous eternal tragedy to come to the end of life with unforgiven sins.

To be forgiven simply means that God has released us (sinners) from judgment and from the penalty of sin, which is eternal death. That is good news, isn't it? Can you think of a miracle more significant than that? God removes our sins from us as far as the east is from the west, and those sins will never come up against us to condemn us in this world or the world to come. That is the greatest miracle of all. That is not a temporary miracle but an eternal miracle. That which is eternal is more valuable than the ephemeral, especially when it is about being forever present with God. Only God can forgive sin. After all, He is the only one without sin.

Those who understand that they are sinners, who have been exonerated of their many sins, love God very much. They know what God has done for them. It was not their love for God that caused their clemency. Forgiveness is a gracious act of God. Therefore, we love God much because He has forgiven much. We appreciate God's forgiveness for our many sins, for without it we are condemned to death forever. Hence, we cannot do anything but love God very much. Do you appreciate God's gracious act of amnesty? Are you grateful that God has removed your sins? Do you love God? To love God is to pick up your cross and follow Him to the place of crucifixion.

6

"For the grace of God that bringeth salvation hath appeared to all men." (Titus 2:11)

There is no reason for anyone to be lost. God has arranged for everyone to be saved. The Bible teaches that it is the will of God that no one perishes. God loves us all. No one is out of reach of His love. No matter who you are, what you have or do not have, God loves you. That is an undisputed fact. God loves every human being not because we deserve to be loved but because it is His nature to love. The Scripture teaches us that God is love; therefore, God cannot do anything but love us. This does not mean that people are automatically saved. It does mean that God has made provision for everyone to be saved. The choice is in the hands of every individual. Perhaps someone is thinking about those who have not heard of the saving grace of God. Will they be lost? I believe that God has even provided a way for them because of His love. Just as God accepts little children, He also accepts those who have not been fortunate enough to hear about His saving grace. If you choose to believe something different, that is your choice. The main focus of this text is that salvation has appeared to all men.

The grace of God that offers salvation has appeared to all men. In other words, the offer of salvation has appeared to us all. God offers salvation to all of us because of His grace. Salvation is an eternal state that none of us deserves. Grace has been defined as God's unmerited favor. God offers us salvation that we do not deserve. God is always showering us with His grace. It was grace that woke us up this morning. It was grace that brought us through danger seen and unseen. It was grace that kept our enemy from taking us out. It was grace that saved us from ourselves. It was grace that kept us from losing our minds. It was grace that caused us to have what we have. There have been sickness and disease that should have taken some of us out, but grace brought us through. We thank God for His grace.

We give God special thanks for His saving grace that is without prejudice. God's saving grace is His most precious and valuable gift of all. If we were able to conquer the whole world but miss out on the grace that brings salvation, all would be in vain. Our greatest hope has nothing to do with the things of this world; it has everything to do with the things of the world to come. To gain this world and miss the next world is to gain an eternal disaster.

Now that I have experienced God's saving grace, my goal for the present is to be more like Him. My blessed hope, which embraces the future, is to spend eternity in His everlasting presence. I am forever thankful for God's saving grace. What about you? Are you thankful for God's saving grace? Does your daily life express your gratitude for His saving grace?

7

"And Abram said unto Lot, Let there be no strife, I pray thee,
between me and thee, and between my herdmen and thy herdmen;
*for we **be** brethren." (Genesis 13:8)*

Can you imagine what it would be like to live in a world without discord? Can you imagine what it would be like if everybody got along with one another? In such a world, there would be disagreement without division and confusion. People would disagree and still work together for the glory of God and the benefit of all of humanity. There would be no hate crimes, no terrorist groups, no gang fighting, and no killings. There would be different organizations and perhaps even gangs, but they would live for the well-being of humankind. People would be mindful of the fact that we are all different but that we are all made in the image and likeness of God, which would result in respect and love for all, regardless of race, creed, or color. This is pure idealism, not realism, because of sin. However, it is this idealistic world that all of us should strive to live in.

It is challenging to live in this world without experiencing strife. Friction seems to be a part of everyday living. There is strife in the home, on the job, in the community, and even in the church. Everyone at one time or another will come face to face with contention. It cannot be avoided since some people are determined to have their way at the expense of others. Turmoil exists because of selfishness, jealously, envy, greed, etc. What's more, some people seem to work hard to bring about discord. It appears that their sole purpose for existing is to encourage disagreement. They are not happy unless they are arguing or causing others to quarrel. Strife is the very reason why some have walked away from their church, their marriage, their community, and even their job.

Conflict, when it is out of control, will often lead to destruction. It will cause people to do and say things they will dread for the rest of their lives.

Abraham knew of the danger that strife was capable of producing. He knew that strife could destroy humans and relationships. He knew that nothing good could come from conflict; therefore, he went to his nephew with an unselfish proposal to avoid strife. In doing so, it proved that Abraham had the best interest of Lot in mind. Abraham did what was not expected: he gave Lot the first choice and then took what was left. Abraham allowed Lot to choose what belonged to him for the sake of peace. He went out of his way to avoid strife. If there was going to be a conflict between him and Lot, Abraham made sure that he was not the cause.

We can't avoid conflict. We need to make very sure that if quarreling is present we are not the cause. We need to make sure that we are willing to go out of our way to keep peace and unity. If, for some reason, we discover that we are the cause of the trouble, we need to make sure that we make every effort to set things straight before the sun goes down. We are brothers and sisters. We are family, and family members should strive to get along.

8

"And the scribes which came down from Jerusalem said, He hath Beelzebub, and by the prince of the devils casteth he out devils."
(Mark 3:22)

When Jesus walked among humankind, He went about doing good deeds. He was always reaching out to help people. He always kept the people's best interests at heart. Even though He is not walking among us physically, He has come alongside us to walk with us daily in a spiritual sense. As He walks with us and lives in us, He always has our best interest at heart. That is good news to know that He is always working on our behalf for our good. Some pretend to be for us but are really against us; that is never the case with Jesus. There is nothing fictitious about Him. He said that He will always be with us. We can take that to the bank. In other words, we can always count on Jesus. He will never let us down or mislead us. He wants the best for us, and He will, until the end of time, do what He can to make it a reality. He cares for us.

Often the things that Christ Jesus does for us are unappreciated. It is a shame that our Lord is perpetually working things out for our good, and we fail to take the time to thank Him and praise His holy name. This is nothing new. People have always taken our Lord's goodness for granted and even associated his goodness with a spirit of darkness. That is precisely what some of the religious leaders did in the days of antiquity. If anyone should have understood Jesus and His works of mercy and grace, it should have been the religious leaders. Instead of supporting Jesus and encouraging the people to follow Him, they did the very opposite. They attributed his works of mercy and grace with demonic activity. They said that He was performing miracles by the power of the devil. They did everything they could do to bring an end to the mighty and miraculous works of our Lord, even at the expense of the people. If anyone should have been thankful, it should have been those religious leaders. After all, they were waiting for the Messiah with great expectation. When He appeared, they did not know how to accept or appreciate Him.

Often today, people do everything they can to try to hinder the good work that God is doing through us. They do not understand who we are, nor do they appreciate the work that we are doing, even though what we are doing will be beneficial to them, their children, and the community. They associate the good work that God is doing through us with selfishness, egotism, fame, and even a spirit of darkness. They often have negative things to say about us. They do not say those things in secret; they make sure we hear them. They are trying to make us stop the work, and some of us do become disappointed and quit. In this case and in every case, we should possess the mind of Christ. Like Him, we are on a divine mission, and we should not allow anyone to turn us around. Like Christ, let us steadfastly set our face to go to Jerusalem to die. Are you determined to stay with the work until the end, regardless of what others say about you or even do to you?

9

*"Declare ye **it** not at Gath, weep ye not at all: in the house of Aphrah roll thyself in the dust." (Micah 1:10)*

When I was a young lad, some of the children in the neighborhood would gather and have a shooting contest. We would line up some matches in the ground and see who could strike the most matches with our BB guns. It was pure joy to see that match burn. Just to hit the tip of the match and make it burn was a sense of accomplishment, but not the ultimate goal. The ultimate goal was to strike the most matches. We would try our very best to strike the most matches. None of us wanted to lose the contest. There is no fun in losing. No one wants to lose. A loser has no bragging rights. In fact, I have never heard of anyone bragging about being a loser. To do so would be foolish. Bragging rights belongs to the winner. It felt downright good to win the contest. It always feels good to do well. There is a sense of achievement in being the best at something. On the other hand, there is a sense of loss, failure, and disappointment in losing.

That is precisely how we should feel about sin. Sin keeps us from living up to the standards that God has set for us. God expects His children to live holy lives, and we should anticipate nothing less. Living such a life should be our goal. We should be striving each day to do our very best and encourage others to do the same. To do anything other than our best is to fall short. In other words, to stray from the path of righteousness is to sin. Sin has a way of disappointing God who made us in His image and likeness. To sin is to go against everything that God is about. Sin not only disappoints God it also grieves Him and causes Him to lament. Jesus wept over Jerusalem. "And when he was come near, He beheld the city, and wept over it." (Luke 19:41) Sin brings great sorrow. It separates us from God—the One in whom we can do all things and without whom we can do nothing. It separates us from one another, which goes against God's plan for humankind. God expects us to live together in unity for His glory and the benefit of others. Sin destroys everything that is good and destroys the best qualities in us.

Sin is nothing to brag about. It is nothing to be glad about. It is nothing to hold on to as if it is good for the soul. Let us stop bragging about sin as if it is something good. Sin is never good even though it might bring a sense of satisfaction to the flesh. We ought to be heartbroken over sin, so much so that we roll over and over again in the dust, which depicts great distress and sorrow. How do you feel about sin? Does your sin lead you to lamentation and repentance?

10

"And when I saw him, I fell at his feet as dead. And he laid his right hand upon me, saying unto me, Fear not; I am the first and the last." (Revelation 1:17)

Fear seems to be running rampant in this world. People from all walks of life are consumed with fear. The rich and the poor, the black and the white, the famous and the uncelebrated, the educated and the ignorant, the old and the young all experience fear. Fear is not biased toward certain people. It is a universal problem. It is with us from the cradle to the grave. It gnaws at us day and night. Only Jesus Christ can set us free from the bondage of fear.

Henri Nouwen was on point when he brought out that those living in the twentieth century are fearful people. The same can be said of people in this century. The sad news is that no one is talking about the perfect love that casts out fear. Instead, each of us tends to focus on our fears which at times can be many. People have all types of fears. There is the fear of failure, the future, nuclear war, rejection, intimacy, success, responsibility, conflict, a particular person coming to power, sickness, death, loneliness, change, and a multitude of other real or imagine potentialities. Sometimes these fears can cause excessive worry even when there is no real danger.

All fears are not wrong. There is a healthy fear; that is, it is for our good. Everyone possesses such fear by nature. It is an innate fear. Such fear can be an aid to our well-being, comfort, knowledge, and health. To ignore such fear puts a person in a dangerous predicament.

On the other hand, many fears are detrimental to our well-being. They rob us of our effectiveness and our happiness. Fear causes us to become immobile or to fight the flow of things instead of reacting in a positive way to the flow of things. Fear is one of our greatest enemies, and it has destroyed many people.

Throughout the Bible, God has comforted His people with the words, "Fear not." In this particular text, our Lord appears to His servant John with the comforting words "Fear not." There was no need for John to fear his difficult situation or any man because the presence of the living Christ was with Him. Just as the crucified and risen Christ was with John taking away his fears, He is also with us doing the same thing. Let us trust in Him who is greater than all our fears. He also gives us comfort, peace, and security amid a fearful situation. Do you trust in Him?

11

*"And when Abram heard that his brother was taken captive, he armed his trained **servants**, born in his own house, three hundred and eighteen, and pursued **them** unto Dan." (Genesis 14:14)*

There is no question about it. We are our brother's keeper whether we acknowledge that fact or not or even practice it or not. When it comes to the family, this is especially true. Family members should always look out for one another. There should always be love and care in a family. Each member should look out for the best interest of the other member. When one member hurts, all the members should hurt. When one member is joyful, all the members should be joyful. Each member should show more interest in the other member than in himself/herself. Selfishness has no place among family members. The family is a support system that prepares each member to meet God and to enable them to live responsible lives. A vital experience with God has everything to do with living a responsible life, which always entails being concerned about the welfare of others.

As we take the time to reflect on the families of today, we notice that something is seriously wrong. There is no longer a sense of community. The words of our Lord are perpetually coming to pass: "And because iniquity shall abound, the love of many shall wax cold." (Matthew 24:12) Love grows cold when our schedule becomes about us rather than God and others. Thinking more about ourselves often leads to confusion and destruction. That is the very reason that families are dysfunctional and abusing and killing one another. That is the reason there is so much hate, stealing, and killing in the world. Sin seems to be on the rise. We seldom hear about some good news. There seems to be more hate in this world than love. The concept of being our brother's keeper is, for the most part, no longer in effect. Sin is on the rise, and many are satisfied with that. The increase of wickedness in the world is concomitant to the loss of love for God and others.

This saga about Abram reminds us that we are our brother's keeper. Whenever our brother—and we are all brothers through creation or family connection or through the blood of Jesus—is in some kind of trouble, whether it is his fault or not, we should be concerned enough to get involved. It should be our desire to make a difference in his situation. Abram could have found many reasons why he should not help Lot. Lot was selfish. He had taken advantage of Abram. He was carnal-minded. He was in an impossible situation, but Abram did not let these reasons keep him from being compassionate toward Lot. When he heard that his brother was taken captive, he immediately went to his rescue.

There is no ambiguity in the Scripture regarding how we should react when our brother is in trouble. Regardless of the problem, we are not to hesitate but immediately do all that is within our power to deliver our brother. Have you seriously and prayerfully considered who is your brother or sister? Doing so will make this world a better place to live. That should be our goal.

12

"And as it is appointed unto men once to die, but after this the judgment." (Hebrews 9:27)

I went to the funeral of a fellow church member. Funerals have always been a sad occasion for me, no matter how people claim that it is a celebration. In a sense it is a celebration, but it is also a sad occasion. Funerals have taken on another kind of atmosphere since my wife of more than thirty-eight years made her transition to be with the Lord. A strange feeling comes over me at funerals that I cannot explain. They are just different now. I often wonder, "Does anyone else feel the same way, or is this unique to me?"

I was at a revival one night, and the preacher spoke from what he said was an unusual topic to preach at a revival, and I agreed with him. His topic was *How to Deal with the Death of a Loved One.* In his sermon, he brought out that many of us are in denial regarding the death of our loved one. He brought out that when we use such phrases as he or she has gone to be with the Lord, he or she has made his or her transition, and other such phrases, it brings out the fact that we are in denial. He went on to say, "They have not gone to be with the Lord. They have not made their transition. They are dead, and they are not coming back. We need to accept that fact. Quit using such phrases, and accept the fact that he or she is dead." And again he said, "They are dead, and they are not coming back."

As he was teaching us his ideology regarding how to deal with the death of our loved ones, I noticed that he was still wearing his wedding band as if his wife was coming back. Do not misunderstand me; I am not trying to suggest that it is wrong to do so. I think that is an individual preference. In light of his topic, there seemed to be a contradiction to me. It seemed to me that he was in denial regarding his wife's death.

Now let me say something about the phrase that I use to speak of my wife Nella's demise. I often use the phrase that she has made her transition. I understand that she died and is not coming back. On the other hand, I know that she is not dead. The body that housed her is dead. Nella, however, is still alive but her existence is on another plane. "We are confident, *I say*, and willing rather to be absent from the body, and to be present with the Lord." (2 Corinthians 5:8) I have accepted the fact of her death, and I know that she is not coming back.

Funerals remind me of the fact that all of us have an appointment with death. There are times when we are late for an appointment. Sometimes we even call in and cancel our appointment. Then, on the other hand, there are those moments when we deliberately break our appointment. Death, however, is one appointment that we cannot be late for, cancel, or even break. That is one appointment that is out of our control. We will keep it whether we want to or not. "It is appointed unto men once to die, but after this the judgment." (Hebrews 9:27)

All of us must die. That is an undisputed fact. Another undeniable fact is that all of us must stand before God. Being washed in the precious blood of Christ saturates all who stand before God with hope. Christ has died for us; therefore, we will avoid spiritual death. Our fore-parents use to say it this way, "He died, I died, and I don't have to die no more." Those who refuse to follow Christ are void of such a testimony. They, too, will live forever, but with their father—the devil. Once they get there, there is no way out. Funerals remind us of the brevity of life. Are you ready to meet God? Will you allow God to catch you with your work undone?

13

"Thus speaketh the LORD of hosts, saying, This people say, The time is not come, the time that the LORD'S house should be built."
(Haggai 1:2)

We should be perpetually busy in kingdom work. There is no doubt about that. After all, there is much work to do. Kingdom work not only prepares us to meet God, but it also prepares people to deal with the present accurately. That is very important because mismanaging the present will always lead to a depressing and despondent future. What we do right now is of supreme importance. We need to wrap our minds around that as if our lives depend upon it, and they do.

Kingdom work focuses on doing God's will rather than one's will. Therefore, it is a prerequisite to stay in touch with God continually. Praying and seeking God's will should become a way of life. It is impossible to maintain the proper perspective about kingdom work if we neglect praying and seeking God's will. Such an undisciplined life leads to making God's work secondary. God's work should never take second place in our lives. There is nothing more important than implementing God's work. It is detrimental to the well-being of humanity to make some other work more important than God's work. No wonder our Lord, Christ Jesus, said, "I must work the works of Him that sent me, while it is day: the night cometh, when no man can work." (John 9:4) Time is running out. Now is the time to do God's work. Whatever God is calling us to do, we must do it now. The opportunity to do God's bidding will not always be before us. Once the opportunity passes us by, it will be gone forever. We cannot call it back. It is not redeemable.

Taking advantage of the time to build our lives and the lives of others will glorify God and expand His kingdom. The time to do this is not tomorrow, not next week, not next year, or not when things are better. The time is right now. Let us make sure that we redeem the time and not waste it.

The most unfortunate thing that is taking place today is that people, as a whole, seem to be wasting time regarding kingdom building. There seems to be more concern about fulfilling a personal agenda than making God's program a reality. The results are catastrophic: (1) Selfishness has replaced altruism. (2) Immorality has taken the place of morality. (3) Spirituality has succumbed to carnality. (4) Personal agendas supersede God's program. (5) Most of all, heaven's joy has turned into grief. Time and again, we let God down. God depends on us to build our lives in such a way that will stand the test of time. It is a disappointment to God when we put our comfort before His will, when we are more concerned about pleasing others than we are about pleasing Him, and when we are more excited about doing great things but neglect to do that which we know He is calling us to.

It is now time to turn back to God. It is time to stop wasting precious time and making excuses. It is time to get our priorities right. It is time to obey God and build our lives as He would have us do. Are you ready to use your time more wisely for the glory of God?

14

"And he saith unto them, Follow me, and I will make you fishers of men." (Matthew 4:19)

These are the words of our Lord, Christ Jesus. He was talking to men who would become His disciples—men who would leave everything to follow Him. These men did not take long to make up their minds to follow Jesus. Immediately, they began to follow Jesus. Somehow, they felt the urgency of the call of Jesus. When people feel the urgency of the call of Jesus upon their lives, it is difficult to refuse. The plain truth is it is easier to follow the call than it is to resist the call. Following the call of Jesus brings blessing to those who answer the call, despite the hardship that may be experienced from answering the call. Not only will they be blessed, but many they come in contact with will be blessed. It is always a blessing to be in the presence of Jesus, and to walk in His pathway.

This call of Jesus is serious. It is a call that involves life and death. Our Lord came into this world to offer us abundant and eternal life. Yes, He has come to offer us life that has meaning and purpose in this world and the world to come: everlasting life. He extends such a call because He loves the world just that much. He desires no one to be lost. This call is about calling people who will show others the way of salvation. I am glad that our Lord loves us the way that He does. He loves us with an undeserved love.

What do you have to do to experience this call of Jesus? You don't have to be rich or famous. You don't have to belong to a particular social club. You don't have to have a certain kind of job. You don't have to live on a specific side of town. You don't even have to belong to a particular race. You don't have to do anything. This call goes out to all. For some, it is a particular call. For others, it is a call by association. If you know Jesus, you cannot help telling others about Him. All of us who are connected to Jesus by His precious blood are fishers of men.

Jesus says to us today, "Follow me and I will make you fishers of men." What does it mean to follow Jesus? It means to become His servant and accept His authority. It means that you are available to Him to pursue His calling. It means that you are striving to walk in His footsteps and becoming more like Him. It means that you are no longer an outsider but an insider. In other words, you have let go of the things of this world and take an everlasting hold on Jesus.

To become fishers of men simply means that we have become partners with Jesus in the work that He is doing in the world and in us. Our Lord is still directly doing some things today. They are called miracles. At other times, He works through us as we engage in kingdom work of all kinds. In other words, to become partners with our Lord means that we are an extension of Jesus on earth. We are His mouth, hands, and feet as we help those in need.

How have you responded to the call of Jesus? Have you ignored the call? Have you put the call off for a later date? Have you decided not to answer the call at all? Have you answered the call by making yourself available to be used by our Lord as He pleases? What are you going to do with the call of Jesus?

15

*"And David and all Israel went to Jerusalem, which **is** Jebus; where the Jebusites **were**, the inhabitants of the land." (1 Chronicles 11:4)*

Life is a gift from God. There is no question about that. We should live life to its fullest; in other words, we are to appreciate life and enjoy life. We should continuously be aware that life comes from God, and we should perpetually give Him thanks for our lives. Giving thanks to God suggests that we are dependent upon Him for life. After all, He is the giver of life. Since life is a gift from God, we are indebted to Him to live our lives in a way that will honor and glorify him, and also live in communion with one another. We are forever accountable to God for the way we live our lives.

Even though life is a gift from God, life is permeated with trouble and difficulties. Sometimes these adverse and troublesome circumstances are solved quickly and without physical, mental, or emotional injury. But that is not always the case. Sometimes they linger for a long time. Nothing we seem to do will decipher the problem. The problem just seems to keep nagging at us and getting on our last nerve. We are caught between a rock and a hard place. The situation seems impossible to solve. The problem is much larger than we are; however, we must keep struggling to overcome because God has given us life to enjoy, and we must take possession of it. A failure to do so will actually cause us to live a defeated life. God never intended for those who are called by His name to live such a life. Therefore, we must have patience and courage to keep moving forward to take possession of the life that God has already given us. Paul was on target when he said, "Work out your own salvation with fear and trembling." (Philippians 2:12b) We must do our part.

That is the way it was with the Israelites. Jebus was a stronghold in Jerusalem that gave the Israelites serious and constant trouble the entire time they had lived in the holy land. The Jebusite fortress overlooking Jerusalem was the last stronghold of Canaanite power that had never been captured.

"And David and all Israel went to Jerusalem, which *is* Jebus; where the Jebusites *were,* the inhabitants of the land." (1 Chronicles 11:4) God had already given them the city. All they needed to do was to tread upon the land. That is what David did. He took possession of what was already his.

Trials and tribulations are an inevitable part of life. These trials and tribulations are not unconquerable. They are only temporary stumbling blocks that will lead us to victory if we hold our course. The good news is that we are more than conquerors through Christ Jesus. He has given us success, peace, comfort, hope, life, and a heavenly home. Let us stop wasting time and energy. Let us stop complaining and feeling sorry for ourselves. Let us take possession of what God has already given us. Let us claim ownership of what already belongs to us.

Have you taken possession of that which God has already given you? If not, what are you waiting on?

16

*"**It is** good for me that I have been afflicted; that I might learn thy statutes." (Psalm 119:71)*

To be afflicted carries the idea of being oppressed, being subdued, and being made to bow down. No one wants to be afflicted. People will do almost anything to keep from being in such a position. There is nothing desirable about being afflicted. Affliction can cause much sorrow and pain.

In some cases, it has caused some people to have a nervous breakdown. It has caused some to deny the existence of God. Others have lost all hope and committed suicide. Affliction has caused people to do all kinds of irrational things.

Sometimes, the same afflictions that drive some people crazy and cause them to do absurd and unfounded things can cause others to take reasonable and well-grounded measures that will benefit themselves and others. What is it about these people that causes them to take different actions when facing similar afflictions? Could it be that the affliction is not as devastating on some as others? Could it be that some people can just take more than others? Could it be that some have a better support system in place than others? All of these things can play an essential role in the way people handle afflictions, but they do not hold the most effective way of dealing with adversity. I believe that it is one's attitude toward affliction that holds the key that determines the outcome of our afflictions.

Attitudes are critical. Attitude has everything to do with one's well-being. If we think that our afflictions are against us, we will feel bad about them and will have all kinds of negative feedback. Those who feel this way seem to believe that their misery is taking them out. They are usually unhappy and live unfulfilled lives.

Otherwise, those who understand that God is somehow working in their affliction for their good in spite of the pain and disappointment will see their affliction as a pathway to a better life—a better life for them and their loved ones. They will allow their affliction to compel them in the direction of living a happy and fulfilled life. No matter what the affliction is or how difficult it may be, they are conscious that God is working their affliction—even if in a way they do not understand—for their good. Therefore, they rejoice and keep on keeping on.

David examined the difficult and painful afflictions in his life that caused him to bow down and surmised that they were good for him. He came to such a conclusion because it was his afflictions that compelled him to study God's Word more deeply. The more he studied God's Word, the more knowledgeable he became of God, and the greater his desire became to have a closer walk with God. He gained much more than he lost through his afflictions. At this juncture, I am reminded of these words, "For our light affliction, which is but for a moment, worketh for us a far more exceeding *and* eternal weight of glory." (2 Corinthians 4:17)

How do you understand your afflictions? Do you think they are against you or for you? Are they bringing you closer to God or putting distance between you and Him? A bad attitude about affliction leads to bad results in life. The right attitude about affliction produces excellent results in life. Have you checked your attitude lately regarding afflictions?

17

"And, behold, a certain lawyer stood up, and tempted him, saying, Master, what shall I do to inherit eternal life?" (Luke 10:25)

Several years ago, I was at a revival service. The evangelist for the week requested prayers for his sister. The cancer had once again invaded her body, and she was not doing well. According to her doctor, the prognosis did not look good. As the evangelist shared this sad story with us, he could barely keep himself together. After he had given a wonderful word from the Lord, the pastor of the church began to pray for the evangelist's sister. The prayer he prayed caused me to almost tremble in my seat. He stood there before God and before us and dared God not to hear and answer his prayer. He demanded that God heal the evangelist's sister. Several times in his prayer he demanded that God heal the young lady. He talked to God as if he was talking to a child, demanding Him to do something. I do understand that the Scripture encourages us to, "Be careful for nothing; but in everything by prayer and supplication with thanksgiving let your requests be made known unto God." (Philippians 4:6) I believe that the key word in this verse is "request." This word carries the idea of asking God for something, not demanding that God does something. There is a huge difference in asking and demanding. This pastor was very demanding in his prayer. Prayer, in general, carries the idea of engaging in a severe and reverent conversation with God. The pastor may have been serious, but there was nothing pious concerning his prayer. As he was praying, I was thinking to myself, "Where did you get such audacity to approach and to talk to God in such a manner? Do you know that you are tempting God?"

There is no ambiguity regarding tempting God (testing God) in the Scripture. The Bible is clear regarding this matter. "Ye shall not tempt the LORD your God." (Deuteronomy 6:16a) "Jesus said unto him, It is written again, Thou shalt not tempt the Lord thy God." (Matthew 4:7) Despite this warning, people still put our Lord to the test. Testing God involves forcing Him to do something instead of trusting Him because of His faithfulness. God has proved His faithfulness to us again and again. Therefore, it behooves us to trust God rather than to tempt Him. His will and His way are to be trusted and obeyed regardless of our lack of understanding. Are you tempting God when you pray? Are you trying to manipulate God for your interest and on your terms?

18

*"Here **am** I; send me."*
(Isaiah 6:8b)

Several years ago, an important person was asked a question about the race problem. I do not remember the exact question the reporter asked, but I will never forget his answer. (This is not an exact quote, but it is close.) "I am not aware that such a problem exists." I thought that was an outrageous and insensitive response to the African American predicament, which is one of undeniable racism. Racism is a present reality, and to deny its existence is to acknowledge that you are deliberately unwilling to do anything about it even though you have declared to be a Christian, which means to be Christ-like. Being Christ-like involves more than attending church and supporting it financially. Being Christ-like suggests that we are our brother's keeper, and that we love our neighbors as we love ourselves. That being the case, how is it possible to go through life permeated with an attitude of apathy toward those who are different? How can you be satisfied with being part of the problem rather than a part of the solution? How can you proudly and apathetically declare that all is well when it is not? This kind of attitude cuts across the divine plan and undergirds bigotry and racism, which is contrary to everything that the Master Teacher has taught us. Such an attitude will never allow us to say to the Lord, "Here am I; send me."

Our Lord is still looking for people that will make up the hedge, and stand in the gap before Him for the land. (Ezekiel 22:30) God is looking for people from all walks of life to stand against corruption in every place and of every kind. There is a need for people to challenge the church, community, government officials, heads of state, and nations to repent of their wickedness and lead them to experience God's saving grace.

For that to become a reality, one must be aware of the present state of things. One must understand that people, in general, are traveling down the wrong path, a path that leads away from the divine plan. But most importantly, we must understand that God is calling us to make a difference. Are you willing to listen to God? Are you ready to trust God and totally commit your life to Him?

There is a great need for people who will speak out for God, stand upon His Word, and boldly make known the desperate need for morality. Morality, not immorality, is the foundation of a stable society. Are you aware of the time in which you live? Have you heard the voice of God crying out for righteousness? Can the Lord God depend on you? Are you willing to cry out, "Here am I; send me!"

19

*"And he builded an altar there, and called upon the
name of the LORD, and pitched his tent there: and there Isaac's
servants digged a well." (Genesis 26:25)*

Can you imagine what life would be like if God had not revealed Himself to us? God has revealed Himself to us through nature, dreams, events, personal experiences, and through His Word. God reveals Himself to us because He loves us, and because He wants us to get to know Him. Coming to know God is our most significant achievement in life. Trying to make it through this world without God is a great tragedy. It means that we are on our own. We are without a guide, protector, keeper, encourager, and helper. In other words, it merely means that we are completely helpless and hopeless. God has revealed Himself to us so that we will be hopeful and confident. We should not take God's revelation of Himself to us for granted, for without it we would be lost entirely.

Our first response to God's revelation of Himself should be worship. That is exactly what Isaac did. He built an altar, called upon the name of the Lord, pitched his tent, and his servants dug a well. He built an altar, which suggests that he worshipped God. Worship is the most important thing that we do. It helps us to keep God first in our lives. God should always be first in our lives because it is in Him that we move and have our being. Worship helps us to stay focused in a world that is entirely out of focus. Worship enables us to keep close to God, who is the source of our well-being.

This world would be a much better place if more people would set up an altar in their lives, or should I say, the right kind of altar. People, by their very nature, will set up some sort of altar. We are worshipping creatures by nature. We will worship God or somebody or something. That is just the way it is. Worshipping at the wrong altar will produce a false sense of security and hypocritical living. Even when it stimulates beneficial deeds, it is usually for selfish motives. Worshipping at the wrong altar will cause people to ignore the fact that we are all made in the image and likeness of God and are closely related to one another. Therefore, racism and separation take the place of love and unification. A meaningless and purposeless life is the result of worshipping at the wrong altar. There are so many today who are good church members but are worshipping at the wrong altar, and that is the very reason they feel no guilt and no need to repent. They have created a god of their liking.

Worshipping at the right altar will cause us to worship the God of creation rather than a god we created. Real worship is not confined to a particular time and specific place but will spill over into daily living. When we leave the place of worship, we will continue to worship as we perpetually talk to God, forever seeking His face, and always engaging in kingdom work that will bring men and women of all races together for the glory of God. True worship reminds us that this world is not our home. We are just pilgrims and strangers traveling through this barren land; therefore, we will not allow ourselves to be rooted in material things. Let us make sure that we are worshipping at the right altar. What altar are you worshipping at?

20

"Put on the whole armour of God, that ye may be able to stand against the wiles of the devil." (Ephesians 6:11)

Several years ago, when our children were just teenagers, I felt deep in my spirit that something was wrong. This feeling was so embedded in my spirit that I was becoming sick at the stomach. I could not put my finger on it, but I knew that something that was not good was going to happen. Those who have children know what I am talking about. I am sure they have felt the same way. Some have identified this deep-seated feeling as a parent's intuition. In the meantime, I was watching my daughter getting ready to go out for the evening. There was something strange about the way she was moving that caught my attention. I cannot explain it, but there was something different about her. This feeling that something was about to happen was getting stronger. As I made my way to check on my daughter to see how she was doing and where she was going, I noticed that she was putting a knife in her purse. I had found that knife a few days ago. It was long, dirty, and rusty. It was so rusty that it was challenging to open it. I put it in the bathroom drawer to clean it up. When I questioned my daughter about what she was doing, she explained to me that she was going to meet a girl who was more than twice her size to fight it out, and that she needed that knife as an equalizer.

I was filled with anger and laughter at the same time—anger because of her unintelligent and dangerous decision. I was overflowing with laughter because she could never get that rusty knife open. I had her sit down so we could talk about her irresponsible decision. After agreeing with me, I asked her to open the knife. She discovered that she could not get the knife open. That is when both of us burst out with laughter. She not only made a bad decision to meet someone for a fight, but she had chosen a weapon that did not work. She realized that there was no way for her to win that fight. The lesson is twofold. Do everything you can to avoid confrontation, but if it cannot be avoided make sure you know who the enemy is and that you have the right kind of weapon.

We are engaged in unavoidable warfare today. The sad news is that frequently we do not know who the enemy is or that we are using the wrong weapons. No wonder we are losing the battle. We are fighting against flesh and blood using terrestrial weapons. Flesh and blood are not our real enemies. "For we wrestle not against flesh and blood, but against principalities, against powers, against the rulers of the darkness of this world, against spiritual wickedness in high places." (Ephesians 6:12) We must put our mundane weapons aside and put on the whole armor of God. The armor has already been prepared for us; we just need to put it on. We would be remiss if we failed to do so for the battle is authentic, and we are Satan's targets. Our battle is against demonic forces of evil in high places. We cannot stand in our strength with our earthly weapons. Only with the armor of God will we be able to resist the enemy, hold our position, and never surrender. It is a fact that Satan is a powerful enemy, but we have no reason to fear him. He is a defeated foe. All we need to do is put on the whole armor of God and stand together as we engage in this spiritual warfare. Are you ready for battle? Have you surrendered your ineffective weapons? Have you identified the real enemy? Are you aware of his battle schemes? Are you determined to stay the course? Have you put on the whole armor of God?

21

"Therefore the Son of man is Lord also of the Sabbath." (Mark 2:28)

These words of our Lord were strange and challenging for the religious leaders to accept. They ultimately rejected them and considered them to be heresy, which meant as far as they were concerned Jesus would receive swift and inevitable punishment from God for uttering such words. It was because of a lack of understanding and knowledge of the Scripture that they interpreted the words of Jesus as heresy. Being governed by their traditions and their understanding rather than God's Word also made it difficult to accept the Word of Jesus as truth.

Whenever people allow human reason and traditions to take the place of God's Word, they will establish a righteousness of their own and do what is right in their sight, even though it may be contrary to the Word of God. Traditions and human wisdom become more important than God's Word. That is the very reason why the church is changing its rules and regulations to accept those things that at one time were unacceptable by the church. The church no longer sees sin as sin. They are calling sin by another name, which makes it acceptable. The church seems to be more concerned about that which is popular by the majority rather than what is right in the sight of God. Some claim that God is much larger than the Bible; therefore, they are constantly adding to it to support whatever idea they want to. In other words, they have concluded that revelation is still open, even though the Bible teaches that it is closed. It is time for those of us who are called by His name to take our stand, quit embracing what is popular, and endorse the Word of God. Jesus Christ is Lord of the Sabbath and the Lord of His Word.

For that reason, we need to stand upon His Word. In the final analyses, only His Word will stand. Man's word will perish.

The religious leaders could not accept Jesus' words about Himself as being Lord of the Sabbath because they failed to understand who He was. He is the Son of God. God created everything through Him, and gave Him authority and power; thus, He is Lord of the Sabbath. That makes Him greater than the law. The Creator is always infinitely greater than what He creates. Jesus has authority over creation. He is superior to all our rules and regulations.

Jesus Christ being the Lord of the Sabbath suggests several things to us. As followers of Jesus, we need to make sure that our traditions are in line with God's Word. We also must forever keep before us that the Christian Sabbath was instituted for us by God. It is a time of rest and worship. We need to stop making it hard for those who are different from us to join our church. Depicting God's love and grace should be a part of our daily living. But most of all, we are reminded that grace has taken the place of the law, and that our rest is in Him.

Jesus Christ is Lord of the Sabbath and Lord of everything else. Is Jesus Christ the Lord of your life? Have you surrendered the control of your life to Him? If Jesus is Lord of your life, you will come to understand that your life is not about you; it is about God and others. We exist to serve God and others. Nothing should ever take precedence over that fact. What are you waiting on to make the Lord of the Sabbath the Lord of your life?

22

"And David was greatly distressed; for the people spake of stoning him, because the soul of all the people was grieved, every man for his sons and for his daughters: but David encouraged himself in the LORD his God." (1 Samuel 30:6)

Often time, trouble, and disaster catch us completely off guard. When that happens, we are usually overwhelmed by the adverse situation. If we are not prayerful and careful, our faith will be shaken for a moment, and we might seriously think of doing something foolish. There are times when we do just that. How many mistakes have you made because you allowed your troublesome condition to control your thoughts and actions? Such a response is seldom rewarding. We should never let unfortunate circumstances govern our thoughts and actions, causing us to become depressed and inactive. Instead, we need to take charge of the situation by responding to the situation. To do so, we must find courage outside of ourselves.

That is precisely what David did when he was overwhelmed by an unexpected catastrophe that knocked him and his army entirely off their feet, stripping them of all hope. When David and his army returned home, they discovered that the enemy had destroyed their city and taken the people captive. They did not know if their families were alive or dead. Things looked hopeless. His men were so disappointed that they seriously thought of stoning David. David was filled with sorrow and disappointment. David encouraged himself in the Lord, while his men concentrated on their grief. David found strength in the Lord.

I have some idea of how David and his army felt, at least to some degree. I know what it is like to be in a seemingly abysmal situation.

While attending American Baptist College in Nashville, Tennessee, some years ago, I was utterly overwhelmed by the hardship of being in college and taking care of my family. What compounded the problem was that I was separated from my family, who lived in Sheffield, Alabama. At this particular time, I commuted every week, and on this specific week I lost sight of God for a moment and began to think about how difficult things were. I was having a hard time trying to find a job to support my family and take care of my tuition. I had no idea how I was going to make it. I decided to share my problem with a friend. I learned from that experience that we need to be careful with whom we share our problems. I desperately needed to hear some encouraging words from my friend. Instead, I was utterly shocked by his insensitive and despairing remark. He looked me dead in the eye and said, "The Bible says that a man that won't take care of his family is worse than a [expletive] infidel. You need to take your [expletive] home and take care of your family." Tears of joy began to flow from my eyes as the Lord God restored my focus to Him. I started to encourage myself in the Lord as I declared to Him with great confidence that I am just big enough of a fool to believe Jesus' words to His disciples that if any man leaves everything for His sake and the gospel that he shall receive a hundredfold in this life and the next world eternal life. (Mark 10:28–29) The time will come when life will turn against you, your friends will disappoint you, and the only way you will find encouragement is to encourage yourself in the Lord.

How do you respond when life seems to turn against you? Do you complain and blame others? Do you feel sorry for yourself and give up, or do you encourage yourself in the Lord?

23

*"Kiss the Son, lest he be angry, and ye perish **from** the way, when his wrath is kindled but a little. Blessed **are** all they that put their trust in him." (Psalm 2:12)*

The word opportunity can be defined as any circumstance that is conducive to favorable outcomes. The most important thing we need to know about an opportunity is that it has the tendency not to hang around very long. It sometimes comes quickly and goes quickly. If we fail to take advantage of an opportunity, we may never get that opportunity again; therefore, we should watch and pray. We should go through each day waiting for opportunities God might send our way. We should also constantly pray for wisdom to take advantage of each opportunity, and not to use them for selfish reasons.

Can you imagine how many opportunities you have allowed to pass you by? Can you imagine what your life would be like if you had not missed that opportunity? You might even wish you could go back and take advantage of that opportunity. The sad news is that you can't do that. We must live with the choice we make, and sometimes living with missed opportunities is not so good. Sometimes they will haunt us as long as we live. Some people regret missing their breakthrough to the degree that it plays havoc with their lives. Somehow, they can't seem to get over it and move on.

Different opportunities come to different people. Some opportunities are better than others. Perhaps, there have been times when you wished that you had the same opportunity that someone else had. If we focus on that too much, we will become jealous and perhaps immobile, that is, we will not take full advantage of those opportunities that are precisely custom-made for us. But there is one opportunity that is before all of us: it is the opportunity to become members of the family of God. There is no greater opportunity. If we allow this opportunity to pass us by we might not regret it in this life, but we sure will regret it in the life to come which has no end.

Let us make sure that we embrace this opportunity with our entire being. Embracing this opportunity calls for humility. Humility carries the idea of submissiveness. We must bow down before Christ, our Lord and Savior. It is better for us to bow down than to be broken down. Bowing before Christ is an expression of surrendering our lives to Him, which is a prerequisite for membership into His family. Refusing to humble ourselves before Christ leads to experiencing His wrath. But if we put our trust in Him, we will be blessed. Do you trust the Lord God? Are you confident that He will keep His Word? If not, "Kiss the Son" while you have an opportunity to do so; that is, trust Him today while He is still in the saving business. Trust Him while He is still withholding His wrath.

24

"I am come that they might have life, and that they might have it more abundantly." (John 10:10b)

What does life consist of? It does not consist of the things that we possess. We can own all the material things this world has to offer and still not have life. Many are successful according to the world's standards and just as miserable as they can be. Riches and fame, luxurious homes, elegant cars, good jobs, and financial security do not guarantee that we will experience life as it is meant to be. There is a vast difference between physical existence and experiencing life as God intends us to. Many are alive but are not living. Life consists of much more than possessions.

Jesus our Lord and Savior came into this world that we might have life. He does not want us to merely exist. He does not want us to go through life without really living life as it is meant to be lived. He wants us to have joy, peace, and security in this life, and the life to come, eternal life. He came into this world to make sure that we have just that. For us to have such a life, He gave His life. His death was not only another death that is common to humankind. His death has an everlasting effect upon all those who trust Him. He gives us life in this world and the world to come where life has no end.

Let us take a look at the life that Christ Jesus came to give us. It is abundant life. Words cannot describe exactly all this life entails for we know that it is life as good as it can be, and it is beyond our wildest imagination. This abundant life that Jesus gives surely includes a life that is much richer and fuller than the life this world has to offer. Everything this world has to offer is ephemeral. It is here today and gone tomorrow. In fact, it could be here today and gone today. What this world has to offer is exactly like the world itself. It is perpetually passing away. This world and what it can offer is not only transitory, but worst of all its final destination is eternal damnation.

This life that our Lord offers is completely different because of its result. The result is not damnation but complete exoneration, which escorts us into eternal life. At this juncture, I must remind you of something that seems to have been forgotten by some; i.e., the abundant life embraces both worlds—this world and the world to come. The abundant life begins in this world the moment we trust Christ, and it continues into the next world. This life is about taking the high road rather than the low road of popularity. Such a life is about denying self and following Jesus wherever He leads us, even if it is to Calvary. This life does not deny the existence of pain and problems. It faces them and makes the best of them. Rather than focusing on our anxiety and issues, we focus on Jesus who is the author and finisher of our faith. He gives us peace amid the storm. Like the psalmist we can cry out, "My cup runneth over," (Psalm 23:5) and, let me add, with His peace.

It is a downright shame and disgrace for anyone to live any other kind of life than the abundant life that Jesus offers. What kind of life are you living? Have you ever taken the time to give it any thought lately? Living any other sort of life ultimately disappoints Jesus, who came and gave His life so we could enjoy and embrace the abundant life.

25

"And when he saw their faith, he said unto him, Man, thy sins are forgiven thee." (Luke 5:20)

What does Jesus see when He takes a look at us? The truth is that we are never out of the view of the ever-seeing Christ. His eyes are always upon us. No matter where we go, we are never out of His sight. There are times when we tend to try and hide from certain people. We don't want them to know our business. Sometimes we try to sneak around and engage in an act we know we should not be involved in. We just might be successful in hiding from others, but every attempt to conceal our actions and thoughts from Jesus will be abortive. It is impossible to hide from Jesus. He sees everything that we do. He even knows our every thought. In fact, He knows our thoughts before they enter our minds. He also knows what we are going to do, even before we participate in the act. Since Jesus sees everything we do and knows our every thought and action, are we comfortable with His piercing look at us?

What Jesus sees as He looks at us is of extreme importance. First, His assessment of what He sees is always accurate. We often make mistakes in our evaluation of other people; however, this is never the case with Jesus. He never makes a mistake. Second, his assessment reveals the truth about the way we feel about Him. Sometimes people think that a particular person's faith in Jesus is as strong as an insurmountable fortress when in reality he/she is putting on a show to receive the praise of others. Jesus never sought the approval of others. He knows what is in our hearts. He knows when we are real; He knows when we are faking it. The best thing that we can ever do is to take a good look at ourselves in the mirror and try our very best to see ourselves exactly as Jesus sees us.

Like the psalmist, we need to cry out, "Search me, O God, and know my heart: try me, and know my thoughts." (Psalm 139:23) We need to see ourselves as Jesus sees us because frequently, when we look at ourselves, we see the person we want to be rather than the person we are. Our view of ourselves is often faulty.

But if we do our best to see ourselves through the eyes of Jesus, we will see the truth about ourselves. We will also have mixed emotions. There will be feelings of disappointment and feelings of encouragement—disappointment because we let Jesus down and encouragement because we will strive harder to keep pressing "toward the mark for the prize of the high calling of God in Christ Jesus." (Philippians 3:14) Whatever Jesus sees in us we pray that it will lead to His forgiveness, which will put more distance between us and the world and draw us closer to Him.

Experiencing Jesus' forgiveness will lead to a different kind of life. You will no longer see life through the lens of the world but through the lens of Jesus. What a difference that will make in your life. Have you experienced the forgiveness of Jesus, the Christ—the Son of the living God?

26

"LORD, who shall abide in thy tabernacle?
who shall dwell in thy holy hill?" (Psalm 15:1)

Sunday after Sunday, people gather from all around the world to enter some type of sanctuary to worship God. They come from all walks of life. They are entirely different from one another. Some are rich, and some are poor. Some are of great status, and others are not well known. Some have good jobs, and some are jobless. Some are faithful church workers, and some are identified as pew members. Some belong to one race and some another. But the one thing that they all have in common is their need to worship God. That is the reason why they gather on this particular day. They feel the need to worship God not just as an individual but with other believers. Somehow, worship gives them a sense of meaning and purpose in life. It is this meaning and purpose that make life worth living. It is this meaning and purpose that keeps us hanging in there when life does not make sense. Worship helps us to stay focused when everything around us seems to be distorted and inexplicable. Worship connects us with divinity, without which we have no hope. Worship unites us with God in whom we move and have our being.

God desires our worship. Over and over again, the psalmists invite us to worship God. This invitation is not for God's benefit. It is for our benefit. God does not need our worship. If we fail to worship Him, He is still God and is not affected in any way. God loves us all, and His desire for us to worship Him is for our good. We are the beneficiaries of our worship of God. Worship is for our good. We ought to be thankful that God has introduced a method in which we can encounter Him in a bona fide way. But frequently we are not grateful, and we take our worship for granted. We rush into God's house for worship without any preparation. We sing, pray, and witness to the truth with our mouth, not with our hearts. Often times our way of worshipping is unacceptable to God. Our worship is in vain.

The psalmist raises the question about acceptable worship. Who can draw near to God with acceptable worship? That is the question of the day. This question suggests to me that our way of worshipping God just might please us but be displeasing to God. This forces us to thoughtfully and prayerfully consider God's answer to the psalmist question—obedience to God and maintaining a life of integrity is the prerequisite for acceptable worship. We must worship God on His terms and not ours. Again and again, we endeavor to force our ways upon God, instead of embracing God's ways. What about your worship? Are you doing it your way or God's way? Only God's way is acceptable.

27

"Then said Jesus to them again, Peace be unto you: as my Father hath sent me, even so send I you." (John 20:21)

The world often talks about peace. Nations often come together to talk about attaining peace. Peace seems to be a constant topic today. People sing songs about peace. Preachers often preach about peace. The Bible, the most important book, and the most popular book that has ever been written, has much to say about peace. People are perpetually searching for ways to establish abiding peace. Despite all of our efforts to find peace, it has a way of eluding us. Peace seems to be a scarce commodity. There seems to be more confusion in this world than peace. Peace is lacking in many homes. It is absent in many communities. It is rare in many churches. It is not present in many countries. Peace is not missing because it is entirely out of our reach. Peace is available to us. It is within our reach. It is downright abashment for peace to be so close to us, and we allow it to pass us by.

Jesus came into this world that we might have peace. This peace that Jesus came to give is more than the absence of conflict. This peace carries the idea of completeness, soundness, and the well-being of a person. There is nothing in this world that can provide us with this peace. This peace comes from the Lord God. Apart from faith in Him, there is no peace. Faith and peace are concomitant. You cannot have one without the other; it is like the two sides of the same coin. God is the embodiment of peace. Therefore, to be at peace with ourselves and with others, we must be at peace with God. This peace is confident assurance in a storm. This peace removes our fears about the present and the future. If our lives are full of stress, we must embrace Christ's peace through the help of the Holy Spirit.

Peace is of the utmost importance when implementing kingdom work. Just before our Lord sent His disciples out to engage in kingdom work, He gave them His peace. He knew that His peace was necessary for them to be effective and steadfast in kingdom work. He was sending them out like lambs among wolves. Only His peace would cause them to be fearless and courageous among wolves as they were commandeered and escorted to Calvary. Those who engage in God's work need God's peace, which will enable them to give off the aroma of peace, even during turmoil. As this sweet aroma of Christ's peace fills the atmosphere, perhaps it will be contagious. Are you giving off such an aroma as you implement kingdom work? Do you have such peace? Jesus will give us such peace if we are willing to accept it from Him.

28

"And, behold, a certain lawyer stood up, and tempted him, saying,
Master, what shall I do to inherit eternal life?" (Luke 10:25)

There are times when people are not serious about a particular issue, but the issue itself is severe. They pretend to be very concerned, but in reality, they have something up their sleeves. The lawyer who came to Jesus with this incredibly solemn question was not serious at all regarding his question. He should have been sincere because the topic he questioned Jesus about was and still is of ultimate significance.

It is an inquiry that every human being should prayerfully and solemnly mull over. There is no place for hypocrisy in the light of this query. There is no room for joking and playing around in the face of this question. This request for information should never be brought up to put someone on the spot, yet that is precisely what this lawyer did. He did not care about the correct answer regarding his question. He just wanted to make Jesus, the One who came to show us the way to life, look bad. It is too meaningful of a question for that. It is a question about our final and eternal destination. It is about spending eternity in the presence of the crucified and risen Christ.

As we turn our attention to this question, it seems that too many are not serious about this matter of eternal life. It appears that people in general are more concerned about this present life than about the ultimate future, that is, life after death. People are doing all they can to make this life better, and we should. We should do what we can to make this life better for ourselves and others, which would really please God. Jesus came to offer us abundant life, which could be identified as life as good as it can be. We must remember the abundant life that Jesus offers includes this life and the life to come. But so many people think only of this life, and they do whatever it takes to make their lives enjoyable even at the expense of others. They live their lives as if there is no tomorrow.

To make matters worse, many who are called by His name are putting more emphasis on this life than they are the life to come. They talk about the life to come, but they live as if there is no life to come. If there were no future life, if this life were all we had, then living for the present would be all right. But since there is life after this life (i.e., eternal life), we would be wise to live this present life in the light of eternity. To live any other way is not only foolish and dangerous; it is also an eternal disaster that cannot be reversed.

The lawyer raised a valid question. It is one of the most significant questions of all time. "What must I do to inherit eternal life?" Eternal life is within all of our reach. I thank God for that. If you miss out on it, it is nobody's fault but yours. Perhaps this lawyer was thinking about something he could do to earn eternal life. It is impossible to earn eternal life. Eternal life is a gift from God. Yet while that may be, there is still something we must do. We must claim this gift of God by faith in the crucified and risen Savior, Jesus Christ. Have you claimed your precious gift? Claiming this gift of God will enable you to live this present life in the light of eternity. Thank God for His precious gift.

29

"And Jesus stood still, and commanded him to be called. And they call the blind man, saying unto him, Be of good comfort, rise; he calleth thee." (Mark 10:49)

So many times in life, someone has gone to their brother or sister for help and was let down because he/she refused to lend a helping hand. Others have gone to organization after organization for some type of assistance and were turned down time and again. There are times when people cannot help us. They are just not able. But on the other hand, when they can lend a helping hand, they refuse to do so because of racism, selfishness, or just plain greed. It is sad when one cries out for help, and no one takes the time to stop and do what they can to relieve someone's heavy burden. The Bible teaches us to, "Bear one another's burdens, and so fulfill the law of Christ." (Galatians 6:2) Whatever that burden is, we are encouraged to do what we can to make their load lighter. In doing so, we not only bring joy into someone's life, but at the same time we fulfill the law of Christ, which is the law of love. "A new commandment I give unto you, That ye love one another; as I have loved you, that ye also love one another." (John 13:34) It is awfully sad that people are not excited about lending a helping hand to those who need it. This new commandment of Jesus seems to be losing ground. People's love toward one another appears to be growing cold.

When Bartimaeus heard that Jesus of Nazareth was passing by, he shouted out again and again for Jesus to have mercy on him. He heard the news that Jesus could make the blind see. The more they told him to keep quiet, the louder he shouted for Jesus to have mercy on him. I have no idea why the crowd wanted him to be quiet. Bartimaeus decided that this was one time in his life that he was not going to be quiet. Being quiet would cost him his blessing. Therefore, he kept crying out for Jesus to have mercy on him. There is a time for everything under the sun. There is a time to be quiet, and there is a time to shout out, and this was not the time to be quiet.

Jesus stopped and stood still, and Bartimaeus got Jesus' attention. Jesus heard his cry and sent for him. Jesus not only stood still, heard his cry, and sent for him; He also restored his sight. Our ancestors had it right when they said, "I love the Lord because he heard my cry and pitied my every groan." (Psalm 116:1) Bartimaeus called out to Jesus again and again, and Jesus stood still. He stood still because He could no longer go on. After all, one of His own was calling Him, and He could not pass him by. He stood still because He was not only responsible for Bartimaeus's existence, but He also loved him. He stood still to keep His word (e.g., He had not come into this world to be served but to serve). It was time for Him to minister to Bartimaeus' need. He stood still because he is merciful and gracious. He stood still because He wanted to allow Bartimaeus to respond to His call. He stood still because Bartimaeus was calling His name.

Are you burdened and heavy laden? Are you facing an impossible situation in which you need a miracle? Have you tried Jesus lately? After all, He is within calling distance. He is very near. The good news is that He is ready and willing to meet your every need. If you just call Him, He will stand still, invite you to come to Him, and meet your need. Call Him; keep calling Him, and you will get His attention. He will come to your rescue.

30

"And they shall build the old wastes, they shall raise up the former desolations, and they shall repair the waste cities, the desolations of many generations." (Isaiah 61:4)

If we are honest with ourselves, we cannot help noticing that our churches, families, and communities have been slowly falling apart over the last twenty years. Church membership has fallen off tremendously. The family structure is constantly falling apart because many seem to think that the family is not worth fighting for. Our communities are no longer vital and vibrant. They have become drug- and crime-infested due to immorality. Children are being born out of wedlock at an alarming rate. Men and women are choosing to cohabitate rather than marry. Too many have chosen a life of drugs and crime rather than endeavoring to use their God-given talent to become a responsible human being and make a positive contribution to society. It seems as if people have forgotten that we should be our neighbor's keeper instead of our neighbor's thorn in the flesh. Selfishness and greed have become the main agenda of the day. It is all about me, myself, and I. No wonder everything around us is falling apart.

Things do not have to continue the way they are going. It is possible to turn things around. It is possible for us to recreate our families, our churches, and our communities. The time to do this is today. Each day is a day that the Lord has made in which He gives us another opportunity to rebuild. It is time for us to throw our agendas out of the window and focus on what God will have us to do. To attain such a focus, we must re-establish and maintain a genuine relationship with God. Any relationship with God that is genuine is one of obedience. It is an undisputed fact that God desires that we have healthy families, churches, and communities. Let us get our act together and initiate a vital and robust building program that will rebuild that which has been ruined, put the new generation on the right path, and influence others to join us in the work. In other words, this innovative program will be contagious. But first of all, let us make sure that we start this new renovating program with ourselves and in our own home.

There is no middle ground here. You are a participant in the new renovating program, or you are not. No one can decide for you. You must decide for yourself. Have you decided to join God's renovating program, which is about making things better?

31

"And Jesus said unto him, Verily I say unto thee,
To day shalt thou be with me in paradise."
(Luke 23:43)

These are the most poignant and precious words that a dying person can ever hear. What makes these words so penetrating and costly is that they were unexpected, unwarranted, and astonishing. No one would have ever thought that the Lord would speak such words to one who was beyond any shadow of doubt guilty and deserved to be condemned to death. These words of our Lord were a bolt from the blue to both the religious and the impious. I can imagine the man to whom these words were spoken was awe stricken beyond description. He knew for a fact, even if no one else knew, what kind of a man he was. He knew that he was a thief. He had spent his life stealing from others. He never considered the trouble and pain he has caused others. He did not care. Being a thief was who he was, and perhaps it gave him a sense of pride. But when he was facing death for his wicked deeds, he had a double epiphany. The first was that he deserved exactly what he was getting because he was guilty. The next was that he was convinced in his heart that Jesus could do something about his condemning situation. Therefore, he cast himself fully upon Jesus and found forgiveness and a new home with Jesus in eternity. Jesus made no mistake when He told the religious leaders that, "Publicans and harlots would go into the kingdom of God before you." (Matthew 21:31) The reason for this is they lacked the epiphany the sinner on the cross experienced. They were righteous and did not need a Savior.

Like the sinner on the cross, we are swiftly accelerating toward death. But unlike this particular sinner, many of us have failed to see ourselves as we are—sinners who deserve to die that eternal death. Instead of acknowledging our sins and shortcomings, we make excuses for them. We say things like, "This is just the way I am." "I am just keeping it real." "This is the way God made me." "I am not that bad." "I am better than Joe Blow." "God knows my heart." These words are expressed without a sense of abashment or remorse. They are said with a sense of pride. This means that we are not going to do anything about them because we are not willing to change. Therefore, there is no need to cast ourselves upon Jesus completely.

It is time for us to wake up and see ourselves as we in actuality are—sinners before a holy God. It is time to cast ourselves upon Jesus and receive His forgiveness. It is time to prepare ourselves to enter the mansion He is preparing for us. It is time to prepare to hear those most poignant and precious words of our Lord in our hour of death, "Today shalt thou be with me in paradise." Have you made preparation to be with Jesus throughout all eternity?

32

"Now therefore hear thou the word of the LORD."
(Amos 7:16a)

During the days of my youth, I remember my mother telling me to do a certain thing. Somehow, I paid her no attention and kept doing what I was doing. Then my mother would call me by my name and say with great seriousness in her voice, "Did you hear me?" Those words always got my attention. I immediately began to do precisely what she told me to do because I knew what would happen if I continued to act as if I did not hear her. To hear my mother meant to do what she told me to do. That is precisely what the word "hear" means. It means to respond positively to what has been said. To hear the word of the Lord means to obey His word.

The million-dollar question is, "To whom are you listening?" Many voices are competing for our attention. There is the voice of the world. There is the voice of family and other loved ones. There is the voice of our peers. There is the voice of the flesh. Then there is the voice of God that speaks through nature, circumstances (both good and bad), other people, conscience, but most of all, through His Word. It seems at times that the other voices are more important than the Word of God. The reason this world has succumbed to evil and immorality is due to the fact that people are being governed by the voices of this world rather than the Word of God. There are so many instances, even in the church, where tradition has trumped the Word of God. Nothing in this world should ever take the place of God's Word. Every other word will have its day in court and will be found guilty of being ephemeral. No matter how you cherish it, it will not last. It is an eternal mistake to build your life around the voices of this world. But on the other hand, the Word of God has no end. "For verily I say unto you, Till heaven and earth pass, one jot or one tittle shall in no wise pass from the law, till all be fulfilled." (Matthew 5:18) The Word of the Lord is the only Word that is worth its weight in gold.

The prophet Amos challenges us today to hear the Word of the Lord. To whom will we listen? Will we listen to the ill-advised words of this world, or will we listen to the prudent and judicious Word of the Lord? Who will govern your life, the world or the Lord? Are you building your life on sinking sand or the Solid Rock? The way of the world leads to destruction. The way of the Lord leads to a joyous life that has no end.

33

"When Jesus heard these things, he marvelled at him, and turned him about, and said unto the people that followed him, I say unto you, I have not found so great faith, no, not in Israel."
(Luke 7:9)

These words of Jesus were no doubt extremely surprising and traumatizing to those who heard them, especially the religious leaders. They were God's chosen people. God chose them among all the races in the world to be His special people and to be a light to the world. Perhaps they thought that God chose them because they were different and better than everybody else. The truth is that they were just like everybody else. God choosing them was an act of His mercy and grace. It had nothing to do with who they were. If that were the case, they would never have been chosen.

It is because God chose them that they began to think more highly of themselves than they ought to. They were exceptionally religious people. They observed the Sabbath and kept all the annual festivals. They attended the synagogue and kept the law. They even prayed several times a day and fasted during the week. They also kept the tradition of men. They were impressed with themselves. If our Lord were going to be impressed by anyone, surely it would be them. After all, they had their religious life together. The truth is that the Lord was not impressed at all by their religious activities. Jesus is never impressed by outward religious form. He often condemned this type of religion. This type of religion often impresses people, but it never impresses our Lord. It is possible to be incredibly religious and faithless at the same time. It is one thing to be religious and another thing to believe that the

Lord will do what He said He would do. It is the latter that causes our Lord to marvel.

An elderly lady who was a great Christian lost her husband of many years. When her pastor visited her, she began to cry out as one who had no hope. Before he could say anything, her son, who was a known sinner, said, "Mom, don't worry about anything; it's going to be all right. God will see you through; just trust God, Mom." I can imagine that that was one of those marveling moments for our Lord. Great faith was expressed by one no one would have expected it from. I often wonder if Jesus has to look outside of the church to find the kind of faith that causes Him to marvel. There is no doubt there are people of faith in the church, but is it that marveling kind of faith? Have you taken possession of such faith? If not, then why not?

34

*"He answered and said, Whether he be a sinner **or no**, I know not:*
one thing I know, that, whereas I was blind, now I see."
(John 9:25)

There are many things that we don't know and will never know about the crucified and risen Christ. There are some things about Him that we will never be able to wrap our minds around. We don't know how He could be the God-man, that is, fully God and fully man at the same time. We don't know how He could have been born of a virgin called Mary. We don't know how He could die for all of our sins. We don't know how He can hear all of our prayers at the same time and never get them mixed up. Like Mary, we must confess that we don't know how these things can be. But, also like Mary, we accept these things by faith. We believe everything that the Bible says about Jesus is true. We can't explain them. They contradict everything we know about humanity. They even defy common sense. Our lack of knowledge about Him does not change who He is. Despite tangible proof, we accept these things concerning Him by faith.

As it relates to the man that was born blind, there were many things that he did not know about Jesus. When the religious leaders questioned him about this man called Jesus, he really could not answer them. There were so many things that He did not know about Jesus. However, he did believe that Jesus was from God because Jesus gave him something he never had before and that was sight. In the history of humankind no one has ever received sight that was born blind, and the blind man's testimony suggested that Jesus was a righteous person. They kept questioning him about Jesus, trying to get him to change his story and give glory to God. But the man held on to what he knew to be an undisputed fact. He did not know for sure exactly who Jesus was, but there was one thing he did know. Jesus had changed his life completely. He declared immediately with great boldness and without any hint of ambiguity, "One thing I know, that, whereas I was blind, now I see." He had met Jesus for himself, and his life would never be the same. There was no question regarding what Jesus had done for him.

There are many things that we don't know about Jesus. There are many questions that we cannot answer. But like the blind man we too have met the Savior, and He changed our lives. Our lives will never be the same. We know that He brought us from darkness to the marvelous light. We, too, were blind but now we see. There are many things that we don't know. But there is one thing that we ought to know for sure, and that is we have been saved. It was Jesus and Jesus alone who saved us. Do you know this one thing?

35

"And many other signs truly did Jesus in the presence of his disciples, which are not written in this book: But these are written, that ye might believe that Jesus is the Christ, the Son of God; and that believing ye might have life through his name."
(John 20:30–31)

The world is full of people who are not satisfied with their lives. Even those who seem to have everything going their way are not happy with the way things are going. That which gives life meaning and purpose is missing. People are doing all kinds of things to make life more fulfilling. They are seeking different employments, changing their peer groups, indulging in the nightlife, becoming members of fitness clubs, getting divorces, reading all kinds of self-help books, and some are seeking a different kind of religion. There have been many famous and infamous people who have turned to other religions to find life. However, these various actions and those other religions may offer a false sense of fulfillment. People choose these different things and religions with absolute assurance that they will lead to life. But in the end, there will only be disappointment. "There is a way which seemeth right unto a man, but the end thereof *are* the ways of death." (Proverbs 4:12)

John, that beloved disciple, shares with us his reason for writing the gospel that is identified with his name. Without any ambiguity, he informs us that his purpose is to convince the world that Jesus Christ is exactly who He claims to be—the Son of the living God. God sent Him into the world that we might have life in this world and the world to come. To experience this life, John encouraged us to believe that Jesus is the Son of God and to make Him the Lord of our lives.

You can search the world over; you can try everything the world has to offer. However, in the words of the "Preacher," "All is vanity and vexation of spirit." (Proverbs 1:14b) If you are looking for life, you must look to Jesus. Apart from Him, there is no life. John affirms that God the Father sent God the Son into this world that we might experience abundant life in this life and the life to come.

John informs us that he did not include every miracle that Jesus performed. He only chose a few of them. He only chose seven of Jesus' miracles under the guidance of the Holy Spirit to convince us that Jesus is the Christ, the Son of God, through whom we receive eternal life. We are in the land of the dying on our way to the land of the living. Have you declared to others lately that Jesus Christ is the Son of God and that He desires to be the Lord of their lives? Only by faith in Christ and His finished work on Calvary can a person attain eternal life. Apart from Him, no one can experience eternal life.

36

"Let the word of Christ dwell in you richly in all wisdom."
(Colossians 3:16a)

There is something in all of us that is responsible for our thoughts and actions. We just don't do things out of the blue. There is a controlling factor behind everything we do. Many things tend to control us at times. That great comedian and actor of yesterday, Flip Wilson, spoke of the great manipulator in his life when he said, "The devil made me do it." I am afraid that so many today allow the devil to be the controlling factor in their lives. When we take a look around us and notice all the terrible, evil, and heartbreaking things that are occurring today, have we surmised that the devil made people commit such horrendous and painful acts? I don't mean to suggest that the devil made them do it, but he is the one who is in charge of their lives. He reigns over their lives. Those who refuse to believe that the devil is real must conclude that some evil force has charge of those who commit such monstrous, excruciating, and inhuman deeds. There is something or someone that has entered into our lives, perpetually manipulating our behavior and forging our attitudes and thoughts about God, humankind, sin, death, and the life to come. The kidnapping and coldhearted brutal murder of precious, beautiful, and innocent little children is the work of evil people who handed the reins of their lives to the devil.

The apostle Paul talks about another driving force that should dwell within us. He says, "Let the word of Christ dwell in you richly." The word "dwell" carries the idea of permanently residing in something. In that light, the Word of Christ should always be at home in us, guiding our every step. It is His Word, which is the Bible, that should be the controlling

71

and guiding force in our lives. It is not enough just to hear the Word; we must allow His Word to become a part of our daily living. The Words of Christ must be so vital to us that no matter what dreadful circumstance we encounter, we can always find comfort and encouragement in the Word. Paul knew exactly what he was talking about when he said: "Let the word of Christ dwell in you richly." (Colossians 3:16a) Allowing His Word to dwell in us will change our entire perspective about this life and the life to come. It will change the way we treat ourselves and especially others.

What are you doing with the Word of Christ—the Bible? Do you ever take the time to study His Word? Do you see His Word as authoritative? Have you surrendered to the guiding principles of the Word? The psalmist declared that God's Word brings charity into our lives when we allow it to guide us. (Psalm 119:9) He also informs us that we can avoid the way of sin by storing the Word within our hearts. (Psalm 119:11) What are you doing with God's Word? The choice is yours. Choose wisely.

37

*"God, who at sundry times and in divers manners spake in time past unto the fathers by the prophets, Hath in these last days spoken unto us by **his** Son, whom he hath appointed heir of all things, by whom also he made the worlds." (Hebrews 1:1–2)*

There are many different religions in the world today. They were started by those leaders who claimed that they had a revelation from God even though the Bible teaches that such revelation is closed. Many of these leaders were and still are very charismatic and persuasive in their teachings. Therefore, it was and still is no big deal to persuade and mislead those who have itching ears. They prey upon those whose lives are unfulfilling and void of the true and living God. Such persons are found among all races, cultures, and creeds. The rich and the poor are also included among such people. They are even found in the church. Now that sounds very strange, but there are some in the church whose lives are unfulfilled and void of the Spirit of God and are easily influenced to leave the church for some other type of religion that has nothing to do with the God of the Bible.

Every person, regardless of his/her status in life, is a worshipping creature by nature. That is a fact, and we must worship something or someone. Throughout the ages, specific individuals have taken advantage of this innate quality in us to worship something or someone and have misled people for their benefit. Such people have somehow failed to be deeply rooted and grounded in the Word of God, which is the only handbook of the church and our true guide. The psalmist got it right when he declared, "Thy word *is* a lamp unto my feet, and a light unto my path." (Psalm 119:105) If more people would take God's Word seriously and stop viewing it as archaic and irrelevant for our time and see it as the authoritative Word of God that is very much germane for our day and time, people would not be so easily misled.

This passage reminds us that revelation is closed since God has spoken in these last days through His Son. The only people we should listen to are those who have a proclamation concerning the Son of God that is supported by the Word of God. Any other word should be rejected. Even if an angel comes with another word, you should account him as accursed (Galatians 1:8). Thank God that He has spoken in the past and is still speaking to us today. He speaks to us today through His Son. His Son has revealed to us all that we need to know about God, sin, life, death, and the life to come. Hear ye Him. Are you listening to Him as He speaks through His Word, or are you listening to those who declare their word?

38

*"And when the woman saw that the tree **was** good for food, and that it **was** pleasant to the eyes, and a tree to be desired to make **one** wise, she took of the fruit thereof, and did eat, and gave also unto her husband with her; and he did eat." (Genesis 3:6)*

Yielding to temptation never pays off in the way a person expects it to. For some strange reason, some people seem to think that the results from refusing to comply with God's revealed will are extremely rewarding. They expect to gain something through insubordination that they would not ordinarily receive for being compliant to kingdom rules. That is the way temptation works. Temptation has a way of hindering our sight regarding reality. It keeps us from seeing the truth. It enables us to focus on temporary pleasures and false securities rather than eternal truths and authentic protection that are offered by the true and living God. Temptation causes us to focus on the right now rather than the future. It is always a serious mistake to focus only on the right now. Life involves much more than the right now. I must admit that right now is the most important moment that we will ever have; therefore, it will behoove us to do things right now that will facilitate us toward a better day. If we are not prayerful and careful, temptation will cause us to focus on both right now and tomorrow based on pretense in lieu of reality. That was the mistake of Eve in the Garden of Eden. She allowed temptation to deceive her. She thought that she was being offered a better way of life when in reality she was being offered the opposite. That is the way temptation is and will always be. It offers something that it can never deliver.

Surrendering to temptation is never an isolated incident. It always involves others directly or indirectly. This particular incident involved

Adam directly for she gave him some of the fruit, and he did eat. Eve was deceived, but Adam was not. He participated with understanding. The result of their action was separation from God. Ever since that day, humankind has yielded to temptation which leads to sin and separation from God. Sin places us in a predicament that is impossible for us to climb out of. It places us in an abysmal situation.

The good news is that God loves us so much that He has a plan that ultimately redeems us. He does for us what we could never do for ourselves. Even though we sin and fall short of His glory, He forgives us and treats us as if we have never sinned through His Son Jesus Christ. If we accept His atoning work by faith, then all of our sins are forever forgiven. The psalmist made no mistake when he said: "As far as the east is from the west, *so* far hath he removed our transgressions from us." (Psalm 103:12) Thank God that He is a loving and forgiving God. He has straightened out what we have messed up. Have you experienced His redeeming and forgiving love? If not, what are you waiting for?

39

"And he said unto them, How is it that ye sought me? wist ye not that I must be about my Father's business?" (Luke 2:49)

The fact that God created the universe and everything in it strongly suggests that He is not only sovereign but that He has a unique and personal plan that He is working out. History is not being governed by chance or osmosis. God is the unseen sovereign behind all of history. This world is not spinning out of control, even though from where we are sitting, it seems that way at times. In a way that we don't understand, God is still in charge and is implementing His plan.

Being cognizant of the fact that God has a plan that includes this universe and everyone in it ought to kindle a burning desire in us to do our very best to discover this plan and become partners with God in executing His plan. That is the most sensible and wisest thing to do. However, that is not the most popular trend people are embracing these days. It seems we are living in a time when it appears that people's agendas are more important than God's agenda. People use most of their time, energy, and money trying to attain their dreams. They give little thought, time, or energy to making God's plan a reality. They do just enough to make them satisfied and to keep from feeling guilty. This is not only true on a personal level but also on a public level. It was God who established the government for the good of the people. Yet those who are in office seldom seek guidance from God but try to please those special groups who were responsible for getting them in office. Even in the church, it seems that personal agendas are more important than God's will. No wonder there is a great falling away from the church and God. People have become too egotistical and worldly-wise to be seriously involved in God's business.

This was not the case with Jesus. We see Him at the tender age of twelve in the temple talking to the learned men of that day. He had accompanied his father and mother to the Passover feast in Jerusalem. When the feast was over, his parents thought that He was among the group as they turned toward home. Soon they discovered that Jesus was missing, and they went back to Jerusalem. They found Him talking with the scholars in the temple. When they expressed their concern for His absence, He unapologetically and respectfully replied that they should have understood He must already be about His Father's business. So should it be with us. Life is too short for us to be about any other business than God's business. Have you been about God's business lately?

40

*"And he said, Take now thy son, thine only **son** Isaac, whom thou lovest, and get thee into the land of Moriah; and offer him there for a burnt offering upon one of the mountains which I will tell thee of."*
(Genesis 22:2)

Time and again, it has been said that our salvation doesn't cost us a thing, but it cost God everything. Since God is love, He cannot do anything but love us. He had to pay an extremely high price because He loves us. Love is not cheap. God loves humanity so much that He desires that none of us perish. It was this desire that caused Him to give the best that heaven had to offer to save us. God had to sacrifice His one and only Son to present us with an opportunity to be saved. That is just how much God loves us. I don't understand why God loves us so, but He does. We don't deserve such love, but because God is gracious and merciful, He showers us with such undeserved love anyway. Can you imagine what life would be like if God did not love us? That thought is terrifying. We would go through life all alone. God would no longer be our Rock in a weary land. Are you not glad that God loves us? I know that I am glad. Nothing can separate us from His precious and everlasting love.

God's love for us cost Him everything. He gave His Son to die for our sins. Since it cost God so much to save us, how could anyone surmise that our salvation does not cost us a thing? That doesn't make much sense. I know that salvation is a gift, and in that light, it doesn't cost us anything. There is nothing we can do to earn it. We cannot purchase it. That is true, but God is expecting something from us in return, and we should be willing to give something in return. I think

David had the right idea when he said: "Nay; but I will surely buy *it* of thee at a price: neither will I offer burnt offerings unto the LORD my God of that which doth cost me nothing." (2 Samuel 24:24) Yes, we should be willing to offer God something in return for our salvation.

God called Abraham and changed his life completely. Abraham had done nothing to deserve such a call and change of life. Abraham could not pay God in any way for what He had done and was continuing to do in his life. However, God did expect something from Abraham. God told Abraham to take Isaac, his only son, and offer him as a sacrifice on a particular mountain. Abraham was obedient to this formidable and heartrending command. The good news is that God intervened and stopped Abraham from slaying his son Isaac on the altar. This suggests that God expected Abraham to be wholly committed to Him, and he was.

God has called us from darkness to the marvelous light. Just as Abraham was committed to God, God expects us to be committed to Him. God wants our commitment. Have you given God your commitment? After all that God has done for us, that is the least we can do.

41

"But thou, when thou prayest, enter into thy closet, and when
thou hast shut thy door, pray to thy Father which is in secret;
and thy Father which seeth in secret shall reward thee openly."
(Matthew 6:6)

I recall early in my ministry, listening to some senior pastors talk about public prayer. One of them was very adamant, condemning all public prayers. He used this particular Scripture to support his belief. As the debate continued, I realized that his conviction about public prayer was set in stone and that the other pastors were wasting their time trying to convince him otherwise. I agreed with the other pastors who taught that Jesus did not condemn public prayer. He was trying to teach us that our prayers should be completely different from the hypocritical religious leaders, who often prayed in public to be seen by others. The motive behind their public prayer life was to make people think that they were more pious than they were. They did more talking to themselves than they did to God. I would guess that many of our public prayers are not much better than those religious leaders of Jesus' day. Many who pray in public may be more concerned about the way they sound and using proper English than they are about getting in touch with God. On the other hand, there is nothing wrong with public prayer, especially when it is done in the right spirit. When it is done in the right spirit, there is power in public prayer. We need to make sure that when we engage in public prayer, we do it with the right spirit.

These words of our Lord are not about public prayer; they are about private prayer. He says, "When thou prayest, enter into thy closet..." He did not say, "If we pray" but "*When* we pray." This suggests that our Lord expects us to have a prayer life. Prayer ought to be a part of our very being. It is extremely difficult to live a vital and fruitful life without prayer. It is difficult to go through this world without prayer. As difficult as it is, some are determined to do just that. No wonder so many people are fainting along the way. They have been cut off from the power source, which is none other than God.

But thank God we have a secret closet we can enter and call upon His holy and everlasting name. The good news is that our heavenly Father sees us every time we enter into our secret closet. Even when we shut the door, He still sees us in our secret closet and will reward us openly. We don't have to worry about people scrutinizing our prayer. We don't have to worry about the way we sound. We don't have to worry about using the right words. All we need to do is pour out our hearts unto God. Can you imagine what life would be like without a secret closet? The secret closet is made to go into. When is the last time you entered your secret closet? The good thing about a secret closet is that it is not localized to a specific geographical location. Wherever you go you can take it with you, and enter it anytime you choose to do so.

42

"And Jesus answering said unto him, Suffer it to be so now: for thus it becometh us to fulfil all righteousness. Then he suffered him."
(Matthew 3:15)

What is your most ultimate concern today? Are your most important interests centered on you at the expense of others? The Book of Judges declares that the people did what was right in their own sight. I am afraid that it depicts the guiding philosophy of many of this day and time. People seem to be determined to do what they think is right. That which is right, according to them, is not that which has been proven to be right throughout the years and that has for its foundation the unchanging Word of God, but rather what they think is right even though it may be utterly contrary to the Word of God. I can understand how those of the world can adopt such a viewpoint, but it is difficult for me to understand how those who claim to be followers of Jesus embrace such an attitude. Jesus clearly said that He was the way, truth, and the life, which suggests that all truth must be in sync with Him and His Word. Therefore, if we want to do what is right, we need to be very sure that it conforms to the Word of God. Any other righteousness is not righteousness at all. The problem with the world and many Christians is expressed in the words of the Apostle Paul, "For they being ignorant of God's righteousness, and going about to establish their own righteousness, have not submitted themselves unto the righteousness of God." (Romans 10:3) Any so-called righteousness, apart from God's righteousness, is no righteousness at all.

The words of Jesus to John the Baptist, "Suffer it to be so now: for thus it becometh us to fulfill all righteousness," (Matthew 3:15) remind us that Jesus' most definitive interest was to do the right thing. Doing the right thing for Jesus at that particular time meant being baptized by John. Shortly after He was baptized, it meant facing the devil's temptation in the wilderness. Still later it meant preaching the gospel and calling people to repentance. After that it meant preparing the disciples to carry on the work after He was taken up. Much later, it meant going to Calvary to redeem humankind. Jesus was always committed to doing what was right.

Just as Jesus was dedicated to doing the right thing, we should also be devoted to doing the right thing, no matter the cost. Are you devoted to doing your thing, your peer's thing, or the right thing? Every child of God should be determined to doing the right thing.

43

"And this day shall be unto you for a memorial; and ye shall keep it a feast to the LORD throughout your generations; ye shall keep it a feast by an ordinance for ever." (Exodus 12:14)

There was a time when Sunday was the most important day of the week, especially for African Americans. Parents would spend a lot of their time preparing their family to enter the house of God on Sunday. The entire family would put on their best to enter into the presence of the Lord God. Sunday was a special day, and the church was a special place. Sunday was a special day because it was a day when God's people would come together and worship God individually and collectively. For a moment, people would forget about the troubles of this world and think about how good God is. They would joyfully celebrate God's deliverance from sin and for bringing them through another week. They would make a joyful noise unto the Lord. This joyful noise would be heard from blocks away. People were excited about serving the Lord. Sunday was a special day, and people would gather at the church to worship the true and living God. They were excited about hearing a word from the Lord to help them deal with their predicament. The words of the psalmist were a vital reality, "I was glad when they said unto me, Let us go into the house of the LORD." (Psalm 122:1) All the major businesses were closed on Sunday. It was against the law to sell alcoholic beverages on Sunday. Sunday was a day of reverence, and people respected it to a certain degree. Families would look forward to coming together for Sunday dinner. There was a time when Sunday was a special day. It was a day of worship, rest, and celebration.

But in this day and time, it seems as if Sunday is not so special anymore. The memorial and festive aspects of Sunday that we should keep forever have not been wholly lost, but they do not seem to be as vital as they once were. All the major businesses are open on Sunday. Alcoholic beverages are sold in many cities. People don't go to church the way they used to. Many of those who do go to church seem to be more excited about what they are going to do after church than what they do in church. Perhaps that is part of the reason that the spiritual fire does not burn the way it used to. Of the few who attend church, many want to hurry through the service. They want the service to be as short as possible. They don't want the choir to sing too long. They don't want the preacher to preach too long. They are not too excited about the preached Word because they are more interested in those self-help books than the preached Word. They cannot wait to leave the church and get on with their business, which has nothing to do with associating Sunday with a memorial and festivity to the Lord.

The truth is that this attitude has cost us dearly. We have raised a generation that does not know the Lord. Crime is on the rise. Morality is at low ebb. People not only disrespect the Lord's Day, but they disrespect the Lord Himself. Where do you fit in this equation?

44

*"The LORD **is** my shepherd; I shall not want" (Psalm 23:1).*

From the moment that we are born until the moment of death, we are dependent individuals. That is the inevitable predicament of humanity. No one can reach that point in life where he/she is entirely independent. It makes no difference what one can gain in life; absolute independence is impossible. We often talk about being independent; we even strive to be independent. We teach our children to be independent. All that is good. We should work toward being independent, but total independence is only a figment of one's imagination. There is always the need to be loved and to have friends. We are dependent upon certain people for our education, security, medical care, legal advice, jobs, etc. The idea of going through life without depending on something or someone is enormously ridiculous. No one can go through life alone. Now, the million-dollar question is: Since I was never created to be an independent person but an interdependent individual, who or what should I depend upon? The answer to that question will make all the difference in one's life. It will shape one's entire attitude about life and death.

In this psalm, David shares with us the right answer about whom we should depend upon as we go through life. He unapologetically and unabashedly declares, "The Lord is my Shepherd; I shall not want." David, being a shepherd himself, understood what it meant to be a shepherd. He knew that a shepherd loved, cared for, protected, guided, and comforted his sheep. The shepherd took it upon himself to take care of the sheep, even at the cost of his life. He made sure that the sheep had everything they needed; therefore, they would lack nothing. This is what God was to David. He was everything that David needed; that is the reason he cried out, "The Lord is my Shepherd; I shall not want." David was completely leaning and depending on God to be everything David needed.

What about you? Who are you leaning and depending upon? Do you depend upon your loved ones, friends, or the things of this world? I am not suggesting that we should not depend upon our loved ones, friends, or the things of this world. God has blessed us with people and things to enjoy and rely upon to a certain degree, but to allow our dependency on them to take the place of our reliance on God is a great sin. Nothing should take the place of our dependence on God. Are you totally depending upon God to be everything you need? If so, then you can declare with David, "The Lord is my Shepherd; I shall not want." That is the right place to be in life. Are you there?

45

"Then saith he unto his disciples, The harvest truly is plenteous,
but the labourers are few; Pray ye therefore the Lord of the harvest,
that he will send forth labourers into his harvest."
(Matthew 9:37–38)

How do you feel about your church? How do you feel about the church in general? Do you really care for the church of the crucified and risen Christ? I think that sometimes those of us who attend church regularly take the church for granted. We don't do very much regarding its spiritual health. It is a proven fact that we don't do the best we can financially. Yes, we give enough to satisfy our guilty conscience. Our Lord established the church not for His benefit but for our spiritual, physical, emotional, and mental well-being. In that light, we should not take the church for granted, but we should love the church so much that we become good stewards of the church. The Lord has left His church in our hands to a certain degree; therefore, He is expecting us to take care of His church until He comes back for His church. The church is not just in the hands of the pastor and leaders of the church; it is in the hands of all of its members. We are all responsible for the well-being of the church.

Jesus had been busy going about teaching and preaching about the kingdom of God. Our Lord was always busy. He never wasted His time doing nothing or doing things He should not be doing. He was dedicated and serious about kingdom business. As He went about implementing God's will, large crowds followed Him. When He saw the crowd, He was moved with compassion. He saw them as people who were led by leaders who misled them and took advantage of them.

These leaders' main concern was fleecing the people rather than feeding them. The people were unable to help themselves; they had no shepherd to guide and protect them. Their leaders kept them from following the true leader. In response to their helpless condition, Jesus encouraged His disciples to pray to the Lord of the harvest to send workers because the harvest was ready. Additional workers were needed to complete the harvest—what a prayer for the church.

In that light, we should perpetually pray that the Lord send us leaders who are serious about the church. They should be leaders who will feed and lead God's people in the right way. The time is calling for such leaders because the harvest is plentiful. The church needs to examine its prayers concerning the church. The only way to do that is to scrutinize our prayers for the church in the light of our Lord's will for the church. We often talk about praying in the name of Jesus. To pray such a prayer is more than ending our prayer in the name of Jesus. To pray in the name of Jesus is to pray the mind of Christ. We know that praying that the Lord send leaders to guide His church is praying in the name of Jesus, because such a prayer is His will. Are you unendingly engaged in such a prayer?

46

"Then Jesus turned, and saw them following, and saith unto them,
What seek ye?" (John 1:38a)

So many people go through life without a clear goal to work toward.
They seem to always go with the flow of things. Going with the flow of
things is like going on a trip without a destination in mind. It might be
promising and exciting for a while, but when they come to what David
Jeremiah calls "A Bend in the Road" and they have no idea what to do
or which way to go, life becomes frightening and complicated very fast.
They would never think about going on a trip without a destination.
Despite this, many end up going through life without any idea regarding
where they will end up or what it will cost them to get there. That is
the way life is when they decide to go with the flow. Going with the
flow simply means they have no specific or general plans for their lives
because they have not decided what they want out of life. To live such
a life is to live a meaningless and purposeless life, even if somehow it
happens to lead them into fortune and fame. Meaning and purpose
come from having the right plan and implementing it.

Jesus was walking along when John the Baptist identified Him
for the second time as the "Lamb of God." There was something about
hearing that testimony about Jesus for the second time that compelled
two of John's disciples to follow Jesus. They did not just follow Jesus for
a moment or two; they, in fact, transferred their commitment to Jesus.
This says a lot about the leadership of John the Baptist. John declared
that Jesus was the Lamb of God, and they followed Jesus. We must
perpetually remind those who are under our leadership to never lose
sight of Jesus, and always keep Him in their view. The prophet Isaiah

was on point when he said: "Thou wilt keep him in perfect peace, whose mind is stayed on thee: because he trusteth in thee." (Isaiah 26:3)

The Lord, knowing that He was being pursued, turned around and asked them, "What seek ye?" What a question! This was more than a casual question. This question encompasses one's entire life. The answer to this question will determine whether one's life will be useful or wasteful. Behind this question is the impeccable idea that everyone ought to know what he/she is looking for in life. Too many are not looking for anything in particular. They are just wandering about aimlessly in life. They have no plan and no sense of direction. Therefore, they have no real future.

"What seek ye?" How do you answer this question? Do you know what you are seeking in life? Do you have a plan to implement that will bring fulfillment? Behind every successful story, you will find a plan. Now that you know what you want, and have a plan to bring it about, let me strike a chord. Jeremiah 29:11 reminds us that God has a plan for your life, but is your plan and God's plan the same plan?

47

"Lift up your heads, O you gates; be lifted up, you ancient doors, that the King of glory may come in. Who is this King of glory? The LORD strong and mighty, the LORD mighty in battle."
(Psalm 24:7–8)

So many seem to be busy these days making preparations that will hopefully lead to a successful life. Parents know the importance of preparing for tomorrow. They often encourage their children to get involved in some kind of sports or some other activity that will thrust them into a bright and prosperous future. They sacrifice much of their time and energy supporting their children and hoping that they will be one of the few that will make it to the professional level. There are a few parents who support their children academically. They encourage their children to study hard and make good grades. They know the importance of having an education. There is no guarantee that one will be highly successful due to an education, but it is challenging to make it in this world without an education.

Some are continually putting a good percentage of their income into retirement. They don't want to grow old and have to struggle financially through those retirement years. They make sure that if they happen to live long enough to retire, they will be comfortable. On the other hand, there are those individuals who are so busy living for today that they don't even think about preparing for tomorrow. They live as if there will be no tomorrow. Tomorrow will be a reality for all of us—in this world or the next.

The words of this psalm, "Lift up your heads, O you gates; be lifted up, you ancient doors, that the King of glory may come in," (Psalm

24:7–8) reminds us that we need to make preparation not only to succeed in this world but in the world to come. Too often, people are so busy preparing to live in this world that they neglect to prepare for the world to come. The King of glory is coming again. There is no question about that. The only way we can prepare for His future coming is to prepare for His coming into our lives right now. If we plan on living with Him in eternity, we must live with Him right now. We must prepare ourselves and teach our children to prepare to walk with Him daily. It is wise to prepare to succeed in this world, but it is wiser to prepare for the world to come. Our Lord is on His way back. Are you ready to meet Him? Have you done your best to encourage your children and others to prepare to meet the King of glory?

48

"And he said unto them, Come ye yourselves apart into a desert place, and rest a while: for there were many coming and going, and they had no leisure so much as to eat." (Mark 6:31)

We live in an action-oriented world. We were taught that an idle mind is the devil's workshop. The idea behind that saying is that we should always be busy. We have been taught against being lazy all of our lives. Lazy people don't go very far in life. We have heard many stories about the misfortune of lazy people. To be lazy is to be irresponsible and apathetic about life. It is to live life without any sense of accountability to God, to others, and to oneself. No one likes being around lazy people because they always have their hands out. Those who are lazy do not have much of a future. We have been taught against being lazy.

It is busy and hard-working people that are successful in life. We cannot gain anything by sitting around and hoping that something good will happen to us. We must go and get it. That is just the way life is. We must continue to work hard. It is a good thing to be busy. There is nothing wrong with being busy. The Bible even teaches us to be busy. However, we must remember that there is a significant difference between being busy and being a busybody. The problem with perpetual busy-ness is that it often leads to emotional stress and burnout. When people are experiencing emotional stress and burnout, they tend to do irrational things. Being too busy will also cause people to miss out on those things that are of utmost importance in life. There is no question that Jesus was a very busy person. He never wasted His time. He was always taking care of the work that God sent Him to do. He said, "I must work the works of him that sent me, while it is day: the night cometh, when no man can work." (John 9:4) But He also said, "Come ye yourselves apart into a desert place, and rest a while." (Mark 6:31) Our Lord was very serious about implementing God's work. But He was just as serious about the constant need for rest and restoration of the human body. The work that we have been called to do is more significant than we are. However, we should seriously consider the words of our Lord and "rest awhile."

Does it seem like your world is falling apart, and you are about to have an emotional breakdown? Perhaps what you need is rest. Find that place of solitude where you can rest and relax as you have a little talk with Jesus. A little talk with Jesus will make things better. That is a fact.

49

"Jesus saith unto her, Woman, what have I to do with thee? mine hour is not yet come." (John 2:4)

Throughout the history of humanity, good plans have failed again and again. Just because one has what seems to be an idyllic plan does not mean that people are ready for it and that it is going to work. Timing has everything to do with its success. There have been some poorly designed plans that worked out quite well because they were implemented at the right time. Those who are in leadership positions must understand that timing is of utmost importance. God had a plan to send His Son into the world to redeem it from sin. He just didn't send Jesus into the world at any old time. When the time was right, God sent Him into the world. He did not send Jesus into the world a minute too soon or a minute too late. He sent Him when the time was right. Again, let me remind you that timing has everything to do with the success or failure of a plan. A good idea must be executed at the right time if it is going to succeed. Many leaders have failed because they tried to carry out their plan at the wrong time. The Bible is right: "To everything there is a season, and a time to every purpose under the heaven." (Ecclesiastes 3:1) We must be aware of timing. Sometimes in our zeal we want to implement our God's given plan quicker than He wants it done. That can create a serious problem. Remember that Moses got in serious trouble because he tried to become Israel's liberator too soon.

Jesus and His disciples were invited to a wedding one day. Jesus took great joy in sharing with people in their joyful moments. He was always participating in people's joys and sorrows. That is the kind of Lord we serve. He is still ministering to our needs.

An embarrassing crisis arose. The host ran out of wine. Mary, the mother of Jesus, told Him about the situation, believing that He could do something about it. We need to take to heart the response Jesus made to His mother as He pointed out to her, "Mine hour is not yet come." These words remind us of the fact that timing is of supreme significance to God. God has a purpose for everything in life. He also has His timetable. The poignant query of the day is whose timetable is governing your life. Is it God's timetable or your timetable or is it someone else's timetable?

50

*"Blessed **is he whose** transgression **is** forgiven, **whose** sin **is** covered. Blessed **is** the man unto whom the LORD imputeth not iniquity, and in whose spirit **there is** no guile." (Psalm 32:1–2)*

One of the problems with the church today is that it seems to have lost all sense of guilt for sinning against God and humankind. Somehow the church has found a way to justify its shortcomings. The result is that people continue in their sins without any sense of guilt. They act as if they are not accountable to God for sin. On the other hand, some actually experience guilt because of sin. The sad news is that so many do not know what to do about their guilt. Their little world has been turned upside down because of guilt. They have lost the joy of their salvation. Guilt is a terrible thing to have. It can lead people to despair if it is not properly dealt with.

God created humankind to live in harmony with Him, but this plan failed because of man's deliberate decision to disobey God. The result of this disobedience was that guilt embraced man with its powerful grip and made him a prisoner. At that very moment, a great gulf appeared, separating God and man.

The good news is that despite man being the cause of this separation, God intervened to bring humanity back to Him. When Adam and Eve sinned, they went in the opposite direction from God. They tried to hide from God. They ran from God, but God ran to them. God brought about unification where there was separation. This is the way it has always been; that is, God always takes the initiative to re-establish communion between Him and humankind. Sin makes it impossible for man to restore what he messed up.

The psalmist made no mistake when he declared, "Blessed *is he whose* transgression *is* forgiven, *whose* sin *is* covered. Blessed *is* the man unto whom the LORD imputeth not iniquity, and in whose spirit *there is* no guile." When God forgives us of our sins, we are thrust into a world of unadulterated delight. We are completely blessed; that is, we begin to experience life the way God intended us to. The good news about God's forgiveness is that He completely forgives us. He will never count those sins against us. He treats us as if we have never sinned. What a forgiving God we serve.

Have you placed yourself in a position to receive God's forgiveness? God will not just automatically forgive us of our sins. We must stop trying to ignore or justify our sin if we want to experience the blessedness of forgiveness. The only way to put ourselves in a position to receive forgiveness and be blessed is to possess a repentant spirit. Then we will become that blessed person the psalmist talks about. Have you done just that? If not, what are you waiting for?

51

"And Jesus answering saith unto them, Have faith in God."
(Mark 11:22)

Faith can be defined as a belief in somebody or something. In that light, I can surmise that everyone upon the face of the earth has some type of faith. In other words, they believe in somebody or something. I never met anyone who did not believe in something. It is impossible to go through this life without having some kind of faith. Faith seems to be an integral part of our existence.

People have faith in all kinds of things. Some people have faith in themselves. They seem to think that there is nothing they cannot handle and that they are God's gift to humanity. They are wholly devoted to themselves. They spend all their time and energy on themselves. Some have faith in their jobs. They depend on their job for comfort and security. They never miss a day from work. They dedicate their time and liveliness to their job because that job means everything to them. Then some put their faith in their bank account. They think that their money can buy them whatever they need. They devote themselves to making money and storing it up. It is money that gives them a sense of satisfaction and happiness.

Others have faith in their church. They believe in their church. They act like their church is the only church in the world. Every time the church doors are open, they are there. They never miss a meeting. They hold some type of leadership position in the church, and they are so proud of that. They are faithful to their church, but they somehow don't know how to treat certain members of the church. People have faith in many things. The list goes on and on. It is good to have faith, but we must make sure that it is not misplaced faith; that is, faith that is pointing in the wrong direction. Any faith, no matter how strong and faithful, that lacks a heavenly dimension is misplaced faith. It is this kind of faith that causes people to miss many of the blessings God wants to bestow on them.

In this text, our Lord reminds us of the proper object of our faith. He tells us to "have faith in God." Any other faith is in vain because it is directed toward that which is ephemeral and powerless. Our faith needs to be in Him who is from everlasting to everlasting and who is all powerful. Only faith in God is faith that is worth having and will pay off in this world and in the world to come.

Faith in God carries us beyond the belief of the existence of God. It unites us to Him in an everlasting and significant relationship with Him. What we need more than anything is to be in a real relationship with God. That is what Calvary and Sunday morning is all about. It is about God loving us and us loving Him. It is about a lasting and mutual relationship. Faith in God is the vehicle that leads to such a relationship. Is your faith in God? If so, how has such faith influenced your life?

52

"Jesus answered and said unto him, Verily, verily, I say unto thee,
Except a man be born again, he cannot see the kingdom of God."
(John 3:3)

Any sensible person understands that death is not the end of one's existence. Death is a termination of life as we know it on this side of eternity. This brings out the fact that life continues after death. Now, since life continues after death the most appropriate question is, "Where will life continue?" According to the Word of God, which is the book of the church, there are only two places of existence after death. There is heaven, and there is hell. There are no other places. Heaven and hell are our only choices. We must deliberately choose one of the two. There is no such thing as entering either one of them by accident. The decisions we make have everything to do with how we perceive Jesus Christ, who died to present us with the opportunity to spend eternity in the presence of God. Heaven is the dwelling place of God—the New Jerusalem prepared by God for those who are faithful to Him. Hell is that place of torment prepared for those who are unfaithful to God.

Any sensible person desires to spend eternity with God in that prepared place. The truth is that all of humanity will stand before the God of heaven to be judged. This is one meeting that no one will be exempted from or be late for. The racist, the murderer, the thief, the child abuser, the corrupt politician, the liar, the hypocrite, the adulterer, the self-righteous, etc. will be there. Some will be sent to hell, a place of great torment. Others will be allowed to enter heaven, a place of eternal bliss.

Jesus is engaged in a serious and poignant conversation with Nicodemus, one of the leading religious leaders of that day. The dialogue was about entering the kingdom of heaven. Entrance into heaven has nothing to do with one's good work or qualifications. It has nothing to do with one's religion, but it has everything to do with a radical change from the inside out. We are talking about a new creature, completely new, to be made in a new way. This change is so radical and miraculous that we are wasting our time if we try to bring it about. What is required is a new person. This new person is the work of God and His work alone. Jesus told a particular person that he was not far from the kingdom of God (Mark 12:34), which suggests that we can approach the kingdom of God and at the same time be so far away.

It would do you good to seriously consider your exact location regarding your entrance into the kingdom of God. Are you not far from the kingdom, or are you a very part of the kingdom? If you have not experienced the new birth, you are seriously mistaken in believing that you are part of the kingdom of God.

53

"Therefore all things whatsoever ye would that men should do to you, do ye even so to them: for this is the law and the prophets."
(Matthew 7:12)

These words of our Lord are not new. They have been taught for centuries. Great teachers of the past have taught this principle time and again. The principle of this text runs throughout the Old Testament. It is beyond any shadow of doubt that these words sum up the law and the prophets. We are reminded of how to treat one another. We don't have any problems with technology. We are doing fine in that area. We have no problem when it comes to building great buildings. There are many state-of-the-art buildings to prove that we know how to build. We know how to build highways to make traveling better and faster. We know about flying airplanes and building spaceships that will explore the realm of outer space and go to the moon. We have excelled in mathematics, science, and medicine. The truth is that there are not many things that we do not know about, and we can fix or replace many things that break down. We know how to do great and wonderful things, but we make a mess of human relationships. Families and communities are falling apart because we don't know how to treat one another. Our society is crumbling down because of a lack of comradeship.

We thank God for these costly and relevant words of our Lord for they remind us how to treat one another. Many people know how to apply these words of our Lord in a negative sense. If we do not do to others what we do not want others to do to us, then we are implementing this command of Jesus in a negative sense. If we are going to apply this command positively, we must do more than just refrain from doing something. We must do something good for someone. This will cause us to leave the crowded path and enter into the narrow path that only a few can walk. This is the path that Jesus wants us to take. Such a path will cause us to see a homeless person as we see ourselves—a person made in the image and likeness of God.

Now, the question is, "How do you want to be treated?" Beyond all doubt, you want to be treated with compassion. You want someone to come along and do something about your condition. This is what Jesus is talking about. He is talking about treating someone the same way you would want to be treated if you were in the same predicament. Are you living out Jesus' command in a negative sense or a positive sense? To be cynical is to be filled with contempt. To be positive is to be filled with compassion. It is compassionate people who know how to treat one another.

54

"Jesus saith unto her, I that speak unto thee am he."
(John 4:26)

People go through life searching for meaning and purpose. Meaning and purpose are needed to make life worth living. The reason that so many people go through life with a sense of failure and disappointment is not because of the many overwhelming and lingering tribulations they perpetually encounter. It is not because they were born into poverty. It is not because they were born with some congenital disability. It is not because of racism. All of these things may make life more difficult. They may even immobilize some, hold them as a prisoner, and stop them from moving forward. Some find a sense of satisfaction in blaming some of these things for their failure. People seem to think they are off the hook as long as they can place the blame somewhere else for their failure. Ultimately, these things have nothing to do with keeping us from living a useful and beneficial life. People can be embraced by all of these problems and still have a successful life. People live unfulfilled lives because they have not found anything to give them meaning and purpose for living. They are looking in all the wrong places. They think that meaning and purpose are found in things and favorable circumstances.

The woman that Jesus met at the well was living a life without meaning and purpose. Perhaps she tried husband after husband in order to find meaning and purpose in life, but that did not work out. Her life was still empty. Then she decided to try just living with a man hoping she would find a sense of fulfillment. Perhaps that didn't work out too well, because she was going to the well to draw water when no one would be there. The life she was living was an abashment to her. Thinking no one would be there she went to the well, but someone was there. His name was and still is Jesus. Jesus was the One for whom she had been looking. When she expressed her anticipation of the coming Christ who would tell them all things, Jesus responded, "I that speaks unto thee am he." Finally, the woman had come face to face with the One who could make her life worth living, and Jesus did just that. She went running back to town crying out, "Come, see a man which told me all things that ever I did: is not this the Christ?" (John 4:29)

Have you met this Christ who not only has the power to save you forevermore, but who also has the power to give you meaning and purpose for living? Apart from Him, life is empty and void. Of all the people in your life, you need to make sure that Christ is a part of your life. Have you made sure of that?

55

*"But he **was** wounded for our transgressions, **he was** bruised for our iniquities: the chastisement of our peace **was** upon him; and with his stripes we are healed." (Isaiah 53:5)*

People all over the world are looking for healing. Thousands and thousands of dollars are spent each year by people who are seeking healing. There are times when people have spent their life savings hoping that the doctors will be able to heal them of their disease, or at least give them a few more years. Satan knew what he was talking about when he said to the Lord, "Skin for skin, yea, all that a man hath will he give for his life." (Job 2:4) There are a few people who deliberately decide to take their own life. Somehow, they succumb to despair and conclude that death is the ultimate solution to their problem. But most people will do everything within their power to find healing or a solution to their problem.

I knew of a young Christian man in his early thirties who developed cancer. He hoped and prayed that the doctors would be able to cure him of that dreadful disease. After he realized that the doctors could do him no good, he mustered up all the faith in God that he possibly could for healing, but that was to no avail. He continued to get worse. He even turned to this verse because someone convinced him that this verse was a promise from God to heal all of our diseases. He embraced this so-called promise as much as he could, but he continued to get worse. By this time, he was rather desperate, so he turned to those individuals who claimed that God had given them the power to heal disease. After trying several of them, he continued to get worse. Finally, he died.

The good thing about his death was that he seemed to be at peace with God. But before he accepted the fact that his time had come, he did everything he could do to find healing. People are looking for healing and will do almost anything to be healed.

When Jesus walked upon this earth, He perpetually healed individuals of all kinds of sickness. He was constantly sacrificing Himself for the good of others. Everyone who sought Him out for healing was never disappointed. His healing of physical disease depicted the more profound spiritual healing that Jesus came to perform. Our greatest need is not physical healing, even though it might lead to death. Our utmost need is a spiritual healing that will lead to life, even amid death.

The Scripture declares, "For all have sinned, and come short of the glory of God." (Romans 3:23) Jesus bore our sickness and carried our pain as He hung and died on the cross in our place so that we would have the right to a life where there is no more sickness and death. "But he *was* wounded for our transgressions, *he was* bruised for our iniquities: the chastisement of our peace *was* upon him; and with his stripes we are healed." The wounding, the bruising, and the chastising of Christ heal us perfectly and eternally from all the damage sin has done. Thank God for His precious Son. Have you received the most significant healing of all that He came to give?

56

*"And they that had laid hold on Jesus led **him** away to Caiaphas*
the high priest, where the scribes and the elders were assembled."
(Matthew 26:57)

There is a vast difference in being religious and being a follower of Jesus. The religious leaders of Jesus' day were very religious. They believed in God. They kept the Sabbath Day. They often went to the temple to pray. They gave God their tithes, and they kept their religious laws and traditions. They also spent a decent amount of time studying the Word of God. They were even teachers of the Word. They were members of that nation that God called out and set aside for His purpose and glory. Their primary mission was to lead other nations to God. They were convinced in their hearts that they were special and that they were faithful followers of God. Trying to get them to see the truth regarding their real relationship with God would be as hard as trying to slip daybreak by a rooster. They took their relationship with God for granted. They were convinced that being religious guaranteed them to be in good standing with God. How wrong they were. Being religious and having a real relationship with God are two different things. However, it is possible to be religious and be in good standing with God, but the very opposite is also true.

Before we pass judgment on those religious leaders, let us make sure that we take a good look at ourselves; after all, we could be rocking in the same old boat with them. Let us not take for granted that because we go to church, work in the church, give our tithes and offerings, give to different organizations to help the poor, and maintain a solemn prayer life that we are followers of the crucified and risen Christ. It could be that we are like those religious leaders of antiquity whose religious zeal was, for the most part, about outward performance. It was about looking devout before people. There are many such people in the church and other religious institutions. They are very religious, but they have not developed a relationship with the Lord God.

You can be religious and not know or even care about how to treat one another. But if you are in a real relationship with God, you will know how to treat others. Most of all, you will know how to treat God and His Son, Jesus Christ. Those religious leaders did not know how to treat God's Son. If they had known how to treat Him, they would not have led Him from judgment hall to judgment hall. They would not have lied about Him and condemned Him to death. That is what religious people are about. They are about doing their thing. It is all about them, but they pretend it is about God. They will use and misuse others in the name of God. Where do you stand in this equation? Is it about you, or is it about God? Are you religious, or are you a follower of Jesus Christ?

57

"Ho, every one that thirsteth, come ye to the waters, and he that hath no money; come ye, buy, and eat; yea, come, buy wine and milk without money and without price." (Isaiah 55:1)

God has issued His grand and breathtaking invitation. I am always fascinated by God's invitation because His invitation is entirely different from other invitations that I have seen. God always includes everyone in His invitation. He leaves no one out. No matter what one's status is in life, he/she is always welcome as God's guest. Peter was on point when he said: "I perceive that God is no respecter of persons." (Acts 10:34) God doesn't discriminate based on race, economics, or sex. His invitation is inclusive. That is why I love His invitation so.

But on the other hand, there are those invitations that cannot stand in the shadow of God's invitation. They are very selective regarding who they invite. I can understand that because no one can invite the world to come to their banquet. If money is no problem, a specific location would surely be. With this understanding in mind, social invitations are issued with particular people in mind. Those who don't fit into their spectrum are deliberately left out. The reason for leaving them out varies. I even know of a particular pastor that invites certain types of people to join "his church." I deliberately said "his church" because it is his church. God's church operates based on these unchanging words, "Ho, every one that thirsteth, come ye to the waters, and he that hath no money; come ye, buy, and eat; yea, come, buy wine and milk without money and without price." (Isaiah 55:1)

Black Friday is a time of year when retailers and big brands offer significant discounts on all kinds of products. People stand in lines for hours so they can get the best deals leading up to Christmas. People will go out of their way to get a great deal. A good deal always makes people feel good. Everybody wants a great deal.

God offers the greatest deal of the day, and you would be wise not to miss out on it. Walmart, Target, Best Buy, or Amazon.com never offered a better deal. With God, everything is free. You don't need any money. All that is needed is trust in the Seller, who invites you to come and buy without money. The product that is being sold is not a passing thrill. Instead, it is salvation that comes with a guarantee of complete satisfaction in this world and the world to come. This is the greatest bargain this world has ever known and will ever know. Have you bought into this unparalleled bargain? It is the best deal of the day.

58

*"A new commandment I give unto you, That ye love one another; as
I have loved you, that ye also love one another. By this shall all men
know that ye are my disciples, if ye have love one to another."
(John 13:34–35)*

This world is spinning completely out of control due to a lack of genuine love for one another. The proof that we are living in a loveless society is all around us. It is so apparent that it cannot be denied entirely. I am not trying to suggest that there is no love in this world at all. I am connoting that there seems to be more evidence of the very opposite of love than love itself. The road less traveled seems to be the high road that leads to love. The road most traveled is the low road that leads to hostility, opposition, immorality, and corruption.

People travel the low road because their love has grown cold toward one another. That is the very reason why the family structure, the community, and the church are falling apart. A lack of love causes people to become totally possessed with selfishness which always leads to disrespect and apathy toward the needs and desires of others. It is a lack of love that compels people to develop and maintain a racist attitude toward those who are different. In many cases, life has no real value. Taking a life is as easy as killing some kind of game on a hunting expedition. Notice that I deliberately used the word "game" instead of a dog because there are some who think more of their dog than of certain human beings. Immorality is spreading like wildfire. Many of those who are supposed to take care of our children and guide them along the way are abusing and killing them. The thing that turns my stomach is that parents are engaged in such horrendous acts. At one time, the church was a safe haven, but that is no longer so. When Barack Obama was elected president of this nation, many were disappointed—not because he was not qualified to hold such an office, but because he was different from them. This and many other incidents testify to the sad condition this country is in, especially, in regard to accepting those who do not look like us.

If we are going to reverse the way this world is traveling, we must embrace the command of Jesus to love one another as He has loved us. It is this kind of love that illustrates to the world that we are Jesus' disciples. What do people see when they look at you? Do they see someone who has been with Jesus because of the love you have for others? Let me remind you that love is more than a feeling. It is a mindset that demonstrates itself in action.

59

*"Then one of the twelve, called Judas Iscariot, went unto the chief priests, And said **unto them**, What will ye give me, and I will deliver him unto you? And they covenanted with him for thirty pieces of silver. And from that time he sought opportunity to betray him."*
(Matthew 26:14–16)

Friendship is of paramount significance concerning one's development as a human being. Many individuals' spiritual, emotional, and mental development has been gravely impeded because of a lack of friendship. Having friends and showing ourselves friendly will keep us from being stuck on ourselves. Those who think that everything is about them are usually unfriendly, loveless, and hard to love. Such attitudes are completely contradictory to the nature of our very being. We were not created to keep to ourselves but to perpetually share ourselves with others and allow others to share themselves with us. As we share with others and others share themselves with us, we learn to grow in love. The gratification of sharing for the glory of God and for the benefit of the other can bring the most enjoyable friendships into our lives. Such sharing is impossible in the absence of friendliness. Those of us who follow Jesus should be the friendliest people in the world. We should perpetually reach out to people to encourage them not for our interest but the interest of the kingdom. Friendship is needed to establish and maintain a joyful, peaceful, and stable society.

The friendship between David and Jonathan reminds us of what friendship is all about. There was nothing fictitious about this friendship. It was a genuine relationship rooted and grounded upon trust. David and Jonathan depended upon each other. Each one of them was there for the other in a time of need. They always looked out for the best interest of each other. They were honest and loyal to each other, even though their friendship was risky and costly. The two found themselves in a web of danger because Saul was determined to take David's life and the life of those who helped David. They made a vow and kept it to the end. They never betrayed one another. That is what friendship is about. Their friendship was one to behold and embrace. There is no power in this world like friendship. Friendship should never be taken for granted. It should always be held in high esteem.

Judas Iscariot did not value his friendship with Jesus. Jesus had called him to walk with Him, and Judas spent much time getting to know Jesus. He had witnessed Jesus' unparalleled teaching and saw Him perform miracles. He had even experienced Jesus' love in a very personal way and was given an invitation to become partners with Jesus in the great things that He was doing. Judas should have held on to that special friendship of Jesus with all of his life, but he didn't do that. Instead, he traded that friendship for thirty pieces of silver. In doing so, he became the greatest traitor of all time. I don't know how Jesus felt, but I do know for sure that He felt the poignant sting of betrayal in His heart. Judas turned out to be some kind of a friend.

What kind of friend are you? A true friend will be with you through thick and thin. He will always remain loyal no matter what is going on. Too many people are fair-weather friends. They will hang around as long as they are getting what they want out of the relationship, but when the table turns they will bail out of the relationship. "There is a friend that sticketh closer than a brother." (Proverbs 18:24b) That is the kind of friend that we all need to be.

60

*"But Peter said unto him, Although all shall be offended, yet **will** not I. And Jesus saith unto him, Verily I say unto thee, That this day, even in this night, before the cock crow twice, thou shalt deny me thrice. But he spake the more vehemently, If I should die with thee, I will not deny thee in any wise. Likewise also said they all."*
(Mark 14:29–31)

There are times when we say that we are going to do something with good intentions. It is directly from our hearts without any hidden agenda for personal gain. We want to keep our word because we know that it is the right thing to do. We take great delight in doing the right thing. Keeping our word is of utmost importance to us. God knows that we mean well and will go out of our way to keep our word. The last thing in the world that we want to do is to go back on our word. It is very disappointing when we let others down. When we let others down, we also let ourselves down as well; therefore, we receive a double dose of bad medicine. When we apologize for not being able to deliver what we promised, that does not squelch that awful feeling deep down in our soul. Even when the situation was entirely out of our control, we still regret letting people down. It is a good feeling to know that we have someone we can depend on, and we would like that delightful feeling to be a mutual one. The truth is that we will let others down because we will completely forget about the promise. At other times, something else will occur that is more important to us. Then there will be those times when we are just not able to keep our word. No matter how hard we try, or how desperately we want to do what we promised, we will fail. That is just the way life is.

It is a dangerous thing to be overconfident regarding ourselves. Time and again, the Bible encourages us to trust in the Lord. Peter was warned against being overconfident on the night before he denied Christ. But Peter didn't pay our Lord any attention. He was sure that he would never let Jesus down. He would stand with Him, no matter what happened. He would not only deny the Lord once but would deny Him three times in the same night. Peter had no idea that he was so weak.

I cannot begin to realize how Peter felt when it dawned upon him that he had done exactly what he said he would never do. He denied Jesus three times. Then he began to weep. Peter thought that he was different from the other disciples. In his moment of failure, he discovered that he was no different from them. He needed the Lord's strength just as much as they did. He had to learn how to trust in the Lord and not in himself.

If the work you are doing is your work, then it would be all right to trust in yourself because the work belongs to you. The truth is that the work we have been called to do belongs to the Lord and Him alone. He has allowed you to participate in the work as an act of His mercy. Therefore, put your trust in Him and strive to never let Him down, especially during testing times. When you do let Him down, and you will let Him down in some area of your life, weep as Peter wept. While you are weeping, turn to the Lord and find forgiveness and reconciliation. What a God we serve!

61

*"For the children of Israel shall abide many days without a king, and without a prince, and without a sacrifice, and without an image, and without an ephod, and **without** teraphim: Afterward shall the children of Israel return, and seek the LORD their God, and David their king; and shall fear the LORD and his goodness in the latter days." (Hosea 3:4–5)*

There is no doubt that we are living in the last days. Everything around us is pointing in that direction, especially the world's tendency to lean toward immorality and evil. Things seem to be getting worse as time moves toward the realm of eternity. Time and again, we hear about or witness some unspeakable and unthinkable tear-jerking acts that are pure evil. People are accepting things today that were utterly forbidden and apparently sinful a few years ago. Even though the church is crying out against sin, at least to some degree, the world is becoming more corrupt.

As bad as things are today, one might surmise that things cannot get worse. Some seem to think that our best days are ahead of us. I hate to say this, but they've got it all wrong. Things are going to get worse. If there is any such thing as the golden days, they are not associated with time, but they are associated with eternity. Perhaps you are thinking, "How much worse can things get?"

Just imagine for a moment that people all over the world were separated from their political and religious freedom; that we were living in a lawless society where everyone did what was right in his/her own sight. Everything that reminded us of God was completely removed. We could no longer gather for worship and sing the songs of our ancestors and the new songs of today for the glory of God. Everything we did for the glory of God was contaminated with false worship, no one was serious about obeying God, and the Word of God was considered as obsolete. The only god people were devoted to were the false gods of this world. Such a world is beyond our wildest imagination. We hope and pray that we will never experience such a godless world.

That is precisely what the people of God experienced in the days of antiquity. They had to experience a godless world to come to appreciate living in a godly world. They had to go through a period of the absence of God to learn how to appreciate the presence of God. They had to worship false gods who could not quench the deep yearning in their soul before they would turn back to the true and living God who was able to satisfy the deep thirst in their soul. God had to allow His people to hit rock bottom in every area of their lives to bring them back to Him, where they belonged. What must God allow to happen to you before you give Him your undivided devotion? God loves us so much that He will go out of His way to turn us around. I am thankful that we serve such a God.

62

"If the Son therefore shall make you free, ye shall be free indeed."
(John 8:36)

There is nothing like freedom. Throughout the history of humankind, people have longed to be free. This longing has caused many to give their lives to enjoy freedom. Countries have gone to war to achieve their independence. Freedom has always been the goal of humanity. No one enjoys being a slave. For many, the idea and reality of freedom were much greater than the thought and actuality of death. Many deliberately chose death over slavery; that is, they took their own lives. Others did everything in their power, including risking their lives, to gain their freedom. Many surmised that it was better to be dead than to be a slave. Yes, freedom is worth dying for. This is what Patrick Henry had in mind when he spoke those unforgettable words, "Give me liberty, or give me death!" to the Second Virginia Convention on March 23, 1715, at St. John's Church in Richmond, Virginia. Freedom has never been economical. The price has always been exceedingly expensive. Despite the exceedingly high cost, some were still willing to pay the cost.

Freedom seems to be the ultimate goal in life. The most significant kind of freedom that anyone can embrace is spiritual freedom. Spiritual freedom has come at a great price. What it costs us in comparison to what it cost God who loves us so is like comparing solid gold with ordinary dust. In other words, it is no comparison at all. It only cost us our faith and devotion to Him. Let me add here that our faith does not come from within us; it comes from God. It cost God everything. It cost Him the very best that heaven had to offer. It cost Him His Son, Jesus Christ, who is none other than Immanuel—God with us.

We have been chained and bound by sin without any hope of ever being free from its powerful grip. Only Jesus can set us free from the power and influence of sin so that we can become all that God created us to be. Jesus is the one and the only one that can set us free because He is the very source of truth. Besides Him, there is no truth. He is the standard of what is right. He is the only way into the very presence of God. He does not give us the freedom to do as we please, but the freedom to walk with God. As we strive to walk with God through Jesus, we are free to be all that God is calling us to be.

Are you still a slave to sin, or are you enjoying the freedom that Jesus purchased for you? Are you in the process of becoming all that God created you to be?

63

*"And **so** Pilate, willing to content the people, released Barabbas unto them, and delivered Jesus, when he had scourged **him**, to be crucified." (Mark 15:15)*

There are many people today who go through life doing their best to please other people. Pleasing certain people seems to be their goal in life. They have a great desire to be associated with those they try to please. Belonging to that peer group gives them a sense of identity. It makes them feel as if they are somebody. They will do whatever it takes to satisfy those people in order to become one of them. They never take the time to consider the right or the wrong seriously. They refuse to listen to their conscience regarding what is right or wrong.

We should be thankful that God has given us a conscience that will warn us when we go against His moral standards, but somehow many people tend to quiet their conscience by convincing themselves that they are doing what is best. They also refuse to consider how their actions fit into the plan of God for their life. They are more concerned about belonging to a particular peer group than they are about doing the right thing and belonging to that peer group that John saw, "Which came out of great tribulation, and have washed their robes, and made them white in the blood of the Lamb." (Revelation 7:14b)

The danger of trying to please a specific peer group is that it will cause one to focus on the less important things in life. The things that matter are often overlooked. The temporal becomes more important than the eternal. When this happens, one's destiny is headed in the wrong direction. God's Word teaches us that He will bless those who seek to please Him, not those who seek to please people.

Pilate knew that Jesus was innocent, but Jesus' innocence was not his primary concern. He was more concerned about pleasing the people than he was about doing the right thing. He wanted to be in good standing with the people. It was this misguided aspiration that caused Pilate to ignore his conscience, the Roman law, and warning from his wife about Jesus. Everything in him and around him pointed to Jesus' innocence, but he yearned to please the crowd. That is precisely what he did. He released Barabbas, flogged Jesus, and handed Him over to be crucified.

How do we avoid Pilate's mistake of pleasing the crowd? The way to prevent Pilate's mistake is to pick another crowd. Again, I am talking about that crowd that John saw, "Which came out of great tribulation, and have washed their robes, and made them white in the blood of the Lamb." (Revelation 7:14b) That is the crowd whose main objective is pleasing God rather than man. Who are you trying to please? Pleasing man may bring some temporal blessings, but pleasing God will bring eternal blessings. God is the one to please.

64

*"Bring ye all the tithes into the storehouse, that there may be meat in mine house, and prove me now herewith, saith the LORD of hosts, if I will not open you the windows of heaven, and pour you out a blessing, that **there shall** not **be room** enough **to receive it.**"*
(Malachi 3:10)

How much do you trust God? Perhaps, a better question is whether you trust God at all. Those who are called by His name will declare that they trust God. They not only acknowledge their trust in God but will testify that they trust God for everything. It is one thing to say we trust God, but it is something else to trust Him. Often it is easier said than done. Have you taken the time to prayerfully and thoughtfully consider your trust in God lately? Is what you call trust really trust? To trust in someone means to have complete confidence in someone regarding fairness, truth, honor, or ability. To trust God is to believe that you can entirely depend upon Him to do exactly what He said He would do.

In that light, I would like to say that many trust God for salvation but not for everything else. Some find it extremely difficult to trust God when it comes to their finances. They are willing to use their income to purchase all kinds of things that are not necessary for kingdom living and kingdom ministries. Such things have nothing to do with abundant living. They have everything to do with providing an impressive status for people to behold. We perpetually mishandle our finances and claim that we cannot afford to give to God as we should. Due to insufficient funds, churches all over the world are almost bankrupt regarding doing the work that God is calling the church to do. People come up with all kinds of excuses for not giving to the church. It is time to quit making excuses and trust God with our giving.

People claim that they cannot afford to give as they should, but the truth is they cannot afford *not* to give as they should. There is a blessing in giving, and the truth is that we can't beat God's giving. The more we give, the more He will give to us. God even challenges us to give as we should. God says to prove Him. In other words, test Him and see "If I will not open you the windows of heaven, and pour you out a blessing, that *there shall* not *be room* enough *to receive it.*" Can you imagine that? God will pour out His blessings upon you for your faithfulness until your cup runs over. Are you willing to trust God and give as you should?

65

"And, behold, I come quickly; and my reward is with me,
to give every man according as his work shall be."
(Revelation 22:12)

Those who are in the workplace expect to receive some kind of compensation for their work. They expect the payment to be equal to their work or at least enough to provide for their needs and perhaps a few extravagances on the side. No one expects to work all week without pay. It is just natural for people to expect some kind of reward for their work. The idea of working without some sort of salary is ridiculous. Even when we do good to others, we expect good to follow us. Often, I have heard people say, "What did I do to deserve this?" Such a statement connotes that they expected to receive something better for their service. Their disappointing experience does not match their service. It has been permanently fixed in our minds that what goes around comes around. In other words, good follows good, and bad follows bad. So, as we go through life, we try to live our lives in such a way that good will follow us. I was cutting grass one hot summer day with a push mower. A young man of another race stopped his truck, unloaded his expensive riding mower, motioned his hands for me to move aside, and began to cut my grass. When he finished, he told me, "I try to do a good deed every day. This is my good deed for today. Perhaps, someone will give me a helping hand one day." He expected a reward for his service someday.

The Bible teaches us that the day is coming when we will stand before God and give an account for all that we have done. In this particular text the crucified and risen Lord, our Savior, reminds us that a reward is given to those who have been faithful. Yes, we can expect a reward for our service. Our good work will not be in vain. It is a fact that serving the Lord will pay off in this life and in the life to come.

What is this reward that our Lord promises us? I have no idea what it is. The only thing I know for sure is that this reward is not salvation. Salvation is a gift from God through faith in Jesus Christ. We can't earn or merit eternal life. The reward that our Lord speaks of is a reward for faithful service to Him which always involves serving others for His glory. Even though I have no idea what this reward will be, I know that I will not be disappointed with it. I am looking forward to that day when my salvation is completed, and I will look exactly like Jesus. Not only that, but I am also looking forward to receiving the reward Jesus promised me. What about you? Are you looking forward to receiving your reward?

66

"And the governor said, Why, what evil hath he done?
But they cried out the more, saying, Let him be crucified."
(Matthew 27:23)

Life is full of choices. Making a choice is inevitable. It is impossible to go through life without making some kind of choice. We must decide to choose one thing, person, or course of action in preference to others. That is just the way life is. Some choices are more critical than others. That is the very reason why it is necessary to think through the situation from as many points of view as possible before we make a choice. Some choices will have a lasting influence on our lives that could be good or bad. Some of those bad choices we made still haunt us, but we are still reaping benefits from the good choices. We should never allow the wrong people with the wrong motives persuade us to make a certain choice, especially one that will enable them to implement their agenda. Too many people have ruined their lives and the lives of others by allowing people to influence them to make a decision that would be detrimental rather than beneficial to them in the long run. We need to be very careful to whom we listen. One of the questions that we should ask when confronted with making a choice is, "How will my decision fit into the overall plan of God for my life and the life of those who are close to me?"

The crowd that was persuaded by the chief priests and elders to choose Barabbas and to have Jesus executed did not ask that question. Perhaps, they were convinced that the religious leaders were leading them in the right direction; therefore, there was no need to ask them any questions about this man Jesus. Like so many people, they made their decision quickly with little thought or determination. It seems that they made their decision haphazardly. They made the wrong choice. They chose Barabbas for freedom and Jesus for death.

Pilate knew for a fact that Jesus did not deserve to be crucified, but he did not have the courage to do the right thing which was to set Jesus free. However, he did come up with a scheme to free Jesus, but it backfired. The people chose Barabbas rather than Jesus. Therefore, he gave Jesus over to be crucified.

We all have the right to choose as we please, even if it is the wrong choice. Those who chose Barabbas over Jesus were only exercising their God-given rights. But they made the wrong choice. I thank God that He loves us so much that He gives us the power of choice. We should not take this privilege lightly. Whenever we must make a choice, especially the one about the triune God, we must do so with great prayer and care. Have you made the right choice regarding Jesus? Remember, all decisions have consequences that we must live with or die with. What have you decided about Jesus?

67

"Let not your heart be troubled:
ye believe in God, believe also in me."
(John 14:1)

Trouble is an inescapable quandary of life. It is no respecter of race, age, or status. All will experience trouble in this world. The issue is not if trouble will come but when trouble comes. You can do everything you possibly can to avoid trouble, but it will still enter into your life. No matter how good you think you are, no matter how close to God you are, trouble will come into your life and turn your little private world upside down. It is impossible to live a trouble-free life. Job made no mistake when he said, "Man *that is* born of a woman *is* of few days, and full of trouble." (Job 14:1) When trouble comes, it will make victory feel like defeat. It will make good fortune feel like misfortune. It will make a blissful heart feel like a tormented heart. It will make a molehill feel like a mountain. It will make a vacation seem like active duty. It can make praying seem like empty words. Yes, when trouble comes it has a way of turning your delight into disappointment. Trouble can make a solid foundation seem like sinking sand. It can make hope look like despair. Trouble can turn peace into panic, and shake the very core of your being. Trouble can make you give up when you know you should run on.

These words of our Lord regarding trouble are very precious and comforting to hear, especially to those whose heart is troubled. There is no medicinal cure for a troubled heart. There is a medicine that can numb the heart to a certain degree so that the full impact of the trouble is not felt, but there is no cure. The only hope we have for dealing with a troubled heart is found in the words of Jesus. These words of our Lord make available to us the clue that will enable us to live a life of peace amid a storm.

Jesus understood that His disciples were very troubled regarding the things He had just spoken to them. He wanted them to overcome their troubled hearts. Therefore, He reminded them to continue to trust in Him. The cure for a troubled heart is trust in Jesus. There are many books today that teach the importance of trusting in one's self, that self-confidence is the key to peace. This is contrary to the teaching of Jesus. As it relates to self, our Lord teaches us to acknowledge our weakness and our need for divine help. If we believe that we can make it in life by our strength, we are just setting ourselves up for a great fall. Where is your trust? Is it in you, or is it in Jesus? Jesus is the one in whom we should put all of our trust.

68

*"By faith Abraham, when he was called to go out into a place which
he should after receive for an inheritance, obeyed; and he went out,
not knowing whither he went. By faith he sojourned in the land of
promise, as **in** a strange country, dwelling in tabernacles with Isaac
and Jacob, the heirs with him of the same promise."*
(Hebrews 11:8–9)

Faith is essential to being a Christian. Faith and Christianity are concomitant. You cannot have one without the other. Faith and Christianity are forever bound together. Faith is not a one-time thing. Faith is not a belief in a body of doctrine, even though doctrine is important regarding one's faith. Faith is much more than mere talk. Faith is talk put into action. Such action leads to a personal commitment to Jesus Christ, which in turn is conducive to establishing an authentic and vital relationship with Jesus Christ that is everlasting. Without faith, such a commitment and relationship are impossible. Faith is the key to intimacy with the crucified and risen Christ. "Without faith it is impossible to please God." (Hebrews 11:6) Faith is a continuing process of spiritual growth. Luke describes Jesus' childhood development as growing "in wisdom and stature, and in favor with God and men." (Luke 2:52)

Authentic faith is a faith that produces works that are identified with the kingdom of God. Anyone who claims to have faith but has no evidence of his/her good works does not possess genuine faith. Faith without works is dead. On the other hand, works without faith are dead. Faith and works are concomitant. You cannot have one without the other. We are saved by faith, and that faith enables and compels us to produce good works. Therefore, authentic faith in God is forever evidenced by good works.

We see faith in action in the life of Abraham. He acted upon God's Word even though he had no idea what God had planned. He had no idea where he was going or how long it would take him to get there. All he knew for sure was that God told him to go, and that was good enough for him. He started out on the journey, completely trusting in God and God alone. That is what real faith is about. It is about obeying and trusting in God when we cannot see the entire plan. Abraham trusted God step by step.

Faith is about trusting God regardless of what is going on in your life or how bad things may look. In other words, faith is about trusting in God when you don't know how things will turn out. Faith is not believing that things will work out in your favor. It's believing that things will work out according to God's plan. Faith is trusting God every step of the way. Do you trust God step by step? As we trust God step by step, our faith grows and matures. The focus of our faith is God, and the action of our faith is obedience to God. God always has our best interest at heart. Do you believe that? Is your faith in God?

69

*"In every thing give thanks: for this is the will of God
in Christ Jesus concerning you."
(1 Thessalonians 5:18)*

Too many people go through life with an unthankful spirit. They hardly ever take the time to thank God for His goodness toward them. They seem to think that they are solely responsible for the good things that have taken place in their lives. They are always bragging on themselves. They seldom mention the name of God. It is because of their lack of thanksgiving toward God that they have formed a negative attitude toward life. They complain and blame others when things are not going their way. At times they even have the audacity to blame God for their misfortune. They spend more time thinking about why certain things happened to them rather than taking the time to thank God that things are as well as they are. In fact, they have no reason to thank God because they feel that God does not intervene in their lives. They are hard to get along with and are usually very selfish. And in many instances, they don't feel their very best. Unthankful people are generally not the best people to be around.

Being thankful has everything to do with our attitude toward life. The truth is being grateful is good therapy. When we learn to be thankful in everything, we are on our way to being healthy and happy people. Being thankful enables us to maintain a healthy attitude when life turns against us and when life is in our favor. This is so because being thankful enables us to see every circumstance from a heavenly perspective.

To be thankful in everything is not the same as being thankful for everything. Some things take place in our lives that we should not give thanks for. I once heard a certain man thanking God for his recent heart attack. It could be that he was thanking God for his heart attack because it brought him closer to God. However, there is a difference between thanking God for everything and giving thanks in everything. I don't thank God for the bad and difficult things that occur in my life; however, I have learned to give thanks in everything. No matter what happens to me, I can be thankful because I know that God is with me and because of the good He will accomplish through the adverse situation. God always has our best interest at heart and causes everything to work together for our good. Whatever is going on in our lives, God's got it. It is in His mighty hands; therefore, we can be thankful in everything. Being grateful in everything is a sign that we are trusting in God.

Are you spending all of your time trying to figure out why a particular thing has happened to you? Do you constantly think that it should not have happened? Such thinking will immobilize you. Even if you knew why, it would not change your situation. You think that it should not have happened, but it did happen to you. The only reasonable thing left for you to do is to learn to be thankful in everything. You have unlimited reasons to be thankful. Have you taken the time lately to think about all the reasons you have to be thankful? Instead of trying to figure life out, be thankful.

70

"I thank my God upon every remembrance of you."
(Philippians 1:3)

There is nothing in this world like having a true friend. Elizabeth Barrett Browning once asked Charles Kingsley, "Tell me the secret of your life that I too may make mine beautiful." He replied, "I had a friend." Few of us understand the importance of having a true friend. It is extremely unfortunate to go through life without ever having a true friend. No matter what we accomplish in life, if we have no real friend to share our accomplishments with, they will not mean very much, and our lives will be empty and void. We all need a devoted friend to share things with and who will be there when life throws us a curve.

Don't take friendship for granted. Thank God for your friends. You can go to your friend when you are experiencing family problems. When your little world begins to crumble and fall, and all hope is gone, you can call on your friend. When good and exciting things happen to you, you can share the good news with your friends. Someone said, "Friendship is the great mathematician: It doubles our joy and divides our grief." All of us need friends who will be there for us. You cannot place too much value on friendship. It is extremely difficult to go through life without a friend.

People usually have more acquaintances than real friends. There is a vast difference between a friend and an acquaintance. Acquaintances are people we come into contact with every day. We get to know them and even share some things with them but never on a profoundly personal level. It is usually our job or social activities that bring us together. Such friendship may seem like real friendship, but it is only at a surface level. It will not stand the test of time. In a time of crisis, a real friend can share with us the deeper meanings of these experiences.

The apostle Paul was very thankful for his friends. He knew that they were a gift from God. They came to his rescue time and time again. They were there when he needed them. When the authorities were out to get him, his friends helped him to escape by letting him down over the wall in a basket. When he was stoned and left for dead, his friends were there to rescue him. Time and again, his friends supported his missionary campaign financially. His testimony concerning his friends was that every time he thought about them, he thanked God and prayed for them. Does the thought of your friends compel you to thank God for them and pray for them? It would be good to let them know that you thank God for them and pray for them. Friendship should never be taken for granted.

71

"I can do all things through Christ which strengtheneth me."
(Philippians 4:13)

Those who think more highly of themselves than they ought to often brag about their ability to do anything they want to do. They seem to think that they are sufficient within themselves to accomplish almost anything. They believe in themselves. Such an attitude about themselves is often encouraged by motivational speakers who teach that they can do anything they want if they put their minds to it. It is a good thing to have a firm belief in self-confidence. Such an understanding will enable one to understand his/her limits, look to God for daily strength and wisdom, have a proper concept of himself/herself, and to see others as his/her equal rather than looking down on them. An unhealthy belief in oneself usually leads to an improper relationship with self, God, and others. Such an attitude will cause individuals to do anything they can to get what they want, even at the expense of others. Sooner or later reality will smack them in the face. They will discover their insufficiency during failure. Their great self-confidence will have led them to a great fall.

So many through the years have taken this verse to mean that God will provide them with the strength to do anything they choose to do. The truth is that God doesn't work that way, even though there are times when He will give us the desire of our hearts. The strength that God gives us has everything to do with implementing His will and not our agenda. God will give us the strength to do all things concerning His will and to face the challenges that come from our commitment to carrying out His will. God does not provide us with the ability or the

141

assets to do anything we can imagine that has nothing to do with His will. As we wholeheartedly engage in the work of the kingdom, we will face opposition. Sometimes we may even wonder how we are going to make it. But there is no need to worry because God will not put more on us than we can bear. God will supply us with sufficient strength to do His will.

What does God want you to do? You cannot do it in your strength. It is through Christ alone that you can live a Christian life and accomplish the work. No matter what the circumstances, Christ will enable you to do the work. Therefore, step out in faith and do it, trusting Him for the strength. You can embrace the can-do attitude as long as you are doing Christ's work.

72

"By what authority does thou these things?
And who gave thee this authority to do these things?"
(Mark 11:28)

The word *authority* means "the power to command, the power to issue orders or requisition, the authority to take charge." Everyone does not possess authority. One of the problems we face today is that those who should be following want to be in charge. It seems that some people have trouble following those in authority. I know of an individual who swears that he is a born leader. It was never meant for him to be a follower; at least, that is his claim. He would say unabashedly, "I can't follow anyone because God made me a leader. I am a natural-born leader and not a follower. I set the pace, and people follow me." Somehow, he seems to overlook the fact that one of the qualities of a good leader is that he/she can follow. Usually, those who are self-appointed leaders are more concerned about authority than they are about leadership. Self-proclaimed authority is about accomplishing a personal agenda by having power over people. God-appointed authority is about using that authority to guide, direct, or influence people to achieve a specific goal or end that will honor God and benefit humanity. Authority can be very beneficial when in the right hands. It can be very dangerous when it is in the wrong hands. Even when authority is in the right hands, some have trouble with respecting authority.

Jesus Christ is the ultimate source of real authority. However, the religious leaders disrespected the authority of Jesus. They even claimed that his authority was from the devil. When people disrespect someone's authority, they will bring all kinds of false claims against that person.

They will try to convince others to disregard him/her. Even though the good work that Jesus was doing testified that His authority was divine, the religious leaders did all they could to persuade others to denounce His authority. They were becoming more cognizant of the fact that Jesus' teachings were challenging their authority. To keep their so-called authority intact, they challenged the authority of Jesus.

Do you challenge the authority of Jesus, or do you recognize and respond to the lordship of Jesus Christ? He is not only Savior; He is Lord. In other words, He has been given the title deed to everything we are and all we have. There is no question about it. Jesus should be the grand and magnificent authoritarian figure in our lives. He absolutely deserves to be, because He purchased us not with silver and gold but with His precious blood.

73

*"O taste and see that the LORD **is** good."*
(Psalm 34:8a)

What do you think about the Lord God? Perhaps you think that is a ridiculous and redundant question. The truth is that this is an extremely important and germane question. It is a question that must not be taken for granted or ignored. It has everything to do with how you view this life and the life to come. What you think about God has everything to do with the type of goals you set in life and how you will accomplish those goals. Your thoughts about God determine how you respond to Him in worship and daily living. They also determine how you treat others.

Every person thinks something about God. It is impossible to go through life and have no opinion about God. God is, or He is not. He knows everything, or He doesn't. He is everywhere, or He is not everywhere. He is perfect, or He is not perfect. He can do all things, or He can only do some things. He is completely just and righteous, or He is not. He is absolutely faithful, or He is not. He is with us at all times, or He is not. He is good all the time, or He is not. What do you think of God?

If you have not yet decided what you think of God, the psalmist invites you to try God for yourself and discover that God is good. In other words, you are encouraged to do more than just try the Lord for a minute or two to see if He is good. You are to try God again and again. You are to commit your life to Him, and put your trust in Him, and do your best to receive all that God has to offer. In doing so, you will discover for yourself that God is truly good. Even when the tide of life turns against you, God is still good; He will see you through no matter how great the tide. Have you discovered for yourself that God is good?

74

"In all things shewing thyself a pattern of good works: in doctrine
shewing *uncorruptness, gravity, sincerity, Sound speech, that*
cannot be condemned; that he that is of the contrary part may be
ashamed, having no evil thing to say of you." (Titus 2:7–8)

As children of God, we don't always say nor do what we know to be the right thing. In other words, we sometimes do not set the best example for others to follow. We are guilty of that adage that says, "Don't do as I do, but do as I say." The truth is that axiom doesn't hold any water. If the truth is told, God expects His sons and daughters to do much more than just talk. Something is dangerously wrong when our talk is out of sync with our walk. Just as faith without works is dead, talk without the proper action to back it up is just as dead. Too many Christians are setting a pattern of unwholesome and unsatisfying works. Such works are more in line with the world rather than the kingdom of God. There is a scene in the Bible where Jesus looked out over Jerusalem and shed tears and said, "If thou hadst known, even thou, at least in this thy day, the things which belong unto thy peace! But now they are hid from thine eyes." (Luke 19:42) As Jesus looks out today over the children of the kingdom, I believe He is crying again because we are not setting a pattern of good works. Such irresponsible living has driven a wedge between our Lord and us. It has also caused our testimony to become almost powerless. But most of all, our irresponsible life gives the world the right to say bad things about us and to do so without shame, because what they say about us is accurate.

As children of God, we are encouraged to set a pattern of good works for others to follow. Acts of goodness should characterize us. In other words, our good works should not be done in a vacuum; they should be done in the open so others can observe them. Those of us who are called by His name should not glory in the fact that God is not through with us yet, but we should glory in the fact that we have been changed and live a life that is marked by goodness. Such a life is quite different from those who are disobedient and unfit for doing anything good.

God expects us to set the right example for others. Good talk is empty and void without the proper action to back it up. When people observe that we are striving to become Christ-like, they are far more likely to receive Christ and do their best to be like Him. What kind of example are you setting? Will it lead others to Christ or away from Him?

75

*"And I, if I be lifted up from the earth, will draw all men unto me.
This he said, signifying what death he should die."
(John 12:32–33)*

Our Lord speaks about His death, and what a horrific death it was. It was death by crucifixion which was the cruelest form of execution known to man. It was the Romans who practiced this inhumane form of capital punishment. No matter how notorious a Roman citizen was, he was exempted from its torment and brutality. Such an atrocious and unbearable death was reserved for rebels, slaves, and criminals.

Even though Jesus Christ did not belong to any of these groups, He died such a horrible death. From a human point of view, such a death brings out the wickedness and hopelessness of humanity. There is no limit to the pain people will induce upon others simply because they are different and a threat to the status quo. Jesus was so different and such a threat to the religious leaders' power structure that they decided that He had to die.

Jesus spoke about His death concerning drawing all men unto Him. We know that this does not suggest that everyone will be saved. Some will be lost forever. Our Lord reminded us of this when He said: "Marvel not at this: for the hour is coming, in the which all that are in the graves shall hear his voice, And shall come forth; they that have done good, unto the resurrection of life; and they that have done evil, unto the resurrection of damnation." (John 5:28, 29) The "all men" that will be drawn to Jesus Christ are those who have come to the Light and believe in Jesus Christ. But God will judge and condemn those who refuse to come to the Light.

This inhumane death of Jesus reminds us of the love of God, and what an inconceivable love it is. God loves us so that He sacrificed the best that heaven had to offer. What makes His love so amazing is that we don't deserve such love. Jesus died on the cross not because we loved Him so but because He loved us so. The cross reminds us of how wicked the world is. But at the same time, it reminds us of how great God's love is for us. Thank God for the cross. Without the cross and resurrection, our living would be in vain, and we would have nothing to look forward to when this life is over.

There were three crosses at Calvary. Jesus hung on the middle cross. On one side of the cross, we see a dying thief who reviled Jesus and was lost. On the other side of the cross, we see a dying thief who believed in Jesus and was taken to paradise. Everyone is standing on one side of the cross. What side you are standing on?

76

"All the saints salute you, chiefly they that are of Caesar's household." (Philippians 4:22)

Have you given much thought lately to what being a Christian is all about? I think that the words of Paul sum it up very well: "And be not conformed to this world: but be ye transformed by the renewing of your mind, that ye may prove what *is* that good, and acceptable, and perfect, will of God." (Romans 12:2) Those who follow Jesus have always felt the pressure to follow the script written by the world, but succumbing to such pressure is not allowed. Like those of Caesar's household, we must be victorious over our environment. It is easy to follow the script of Caesar and blame his household for all the ungodliness in our lives. When we do so, we deliberately neglect the authority of Christ in our lives, which reminds us that we have already been given the victory, "Nay, in all these things we are more than conquerors through him that loved us." (Romans 8:37)

Being a Christian is about being victorious over our environment through the crucified and risen Christ. Embracing the ways of the world is taboo for those of us who follow Christ. It is not our goal to embrace as much of the world's way of life as we can and still be a Christian. Our goal is not to be conformed to this world but to be transformed by embracing a new mindset. We must experience a complete transformation from the inside out.

It is possible to live a Christian life despite adverse circumstances. Let me say at this juncture that it is not easy to live a Christian life when the circumstances are unfavorable. During the days of antiquity, many gave their lives. Even today it is dangerous to be a Christian. Many are giving their lives.

Being a Christian in Caesar's household is about being determined to please God rather than Caesar at any cost. We have been challenged to live godly lives in an ungodly world. None are perfect; but we must do the best we can to represent Christ in daily living, which suggests that there are some things that we will not do.

What script are you following—the script written by the world or the Script written by God? Are you living for the glory of God? If so, our light must shine everywhere we go. Christ must be honored in daily living. We can live godly lives in Caesar's household if we are determined to do so. Are you determined to do so?

77

"Bless the LORD, O my soul: and all that is within me,
***bless** his holy name." (Psalm 103:1)*

There is a particular individual that I talk to regularly. It is getting to the point that I don't look forward to talking to him. There are times when I need to hear an encouraging word from him, but that hardly ever happens because he is always complaining about how rough life is. He always focuses on the negative things that are taking place in his life. The only time he ever says anything about all the good things that are taking place in his life is when I bring them up. Then he will simply agree and immediately return to talking about how rough things are. I get so tired of hearing about how rough things are. There are times when I allow him to bring me down; then I have to struggle hard to refocus on how blessed I am. I understand that life can be complicated at times. That is just the way life is. However, I also understand that no matter how difficult life is at the moment, I am still blessed. The good times outweigh the appalling times; therefore, the good times that God blessed me to experience is the dominating theme of my conversation. I don't waste my time talking about how hard life is.

This complaining individual does not stand alone. Many possess the same attitude about life. Such an attitude tends to rob one of his/ her praise. A praise-less life is an unhappy and unsatisfied life. Praising God enables us to focus on the goodness of God rather than our adverse situation. Praising God facilitates strength and reminds us of God's goodness in the past which gives us hope for our present situation.

Those who spend their time complaining would be much better off if they would stop their complaining and spend more time praising

God. After all, we were created to praise God. Like the psalmist, let us encourage ourselves to praise God with everything that is within us. There are times when we must encourage ourselves in the Lord and praise His holy name. Even when we are discouraged or depressed, we have reason after reason to praise God. God is worthy of all of our praise. We were created to praise God no matter what happens to us. It is difficult to praise God when we spend most of our time complaining. Blessings do not come through complaining. Blessings come through praises. When praises go up, blessings come down.

Are you determined to praise God with all that is within you? Perhaps life has turned against you for the worst, and you are having a hard time coming up with a reason to praise God. Dr. Ralph Douglas West got it right when he said: "You can always start with this morning. It was God who woke you up this morning. You can praise God for waking you up this morning."

78

"And as they went to tell his disciples, behold, Jesus met them, saying, All hail. And they came and held him by the feet, and worshipped him." (Matthew 28:9)

Worship is one of the most important things that we do. Both individually and collectively, worship is of the utmost importance. Our individual worship of God does not justify ignoring the worship of God collectively. We have a mandate from God to worship individually and to worship corporately.

Again and again, people have worshipped God according to their own rules. It is God who has established the rules for worship. To ignore God's way and endeavor to worship their way is a sin. There is too much human-made worship taking place in the church today. Many of these worship experiences are weak and shallow. Much of what is done in the church service is not worship at all. It is closer to being entertainment than worship. These people need to get back to the basics and worship God according to the Scripture.

What is worship? As far as I am concerned, worship is difficult to define. I even took a course on worship when attending seminary, and I am still not quite sure how to define worship. I understand that there are some great definitions of worship, but they all fall short as far as I am concerned because there is an element of mystery in worship. Though it cannot be definitively defined, I will attempt to define worship. Worship is the right response to the response that God has made to us. In other words, worship takes place when we become aware of God's manifestation to us in a unique way, and we make the right response to that manifestation. I am convinced that many come to church Sunday after Sunday and never experience a sense of the presence of God. They may feel good. They may even jump and shout. But all is in vain because there is no awareness of God's presence.

The women met the crucified and risen Christ when they were on their way to tell the disciples what had happened. When they met Jesus, He greeted them. They responded to the presence of Jesus by falling at His feet and worshipping Him. Their worship was real. What about your worship? Is your worship authentic? When is the last time that you worshipped God? True worship enables us to keep it real.

79

"And there was a strife between the herdmen of Abram's cattle and the herdmen of Lot's cattle: and the Canaanite and the Perizzite dwelled then in the land." (Genesis 13:7)

Strife is the opposite of peace. Peace should be the ultimate goal of humanity. People all over the world should be striving for peace. However, it seems that most people are putting more energy and time into bringing about strife rather than peace. There is something about strife that seems to make certain people happy, even though conflict always brings about dissension and animosity that may range from a simple difference of opinion to contention and even to violent hostility.

Strife is the inevitable result of selfishness, evil desires, hatred, and anger. It is a vice that is identified with the wicked and is listed in the book of Proverbs (Proverbs 6:16–19) as among the seven things that the Lord hates. The Lord God hates these deadly sins because they keep us from becoming all that God intends for us to become. Let me add at this juncture that this list is not complete, but it does contain specific things that God hates.

The book of Proverbs reminds us that starting strife is like a leak in a dam. Strife starts out small but sooner or later grows big. To cause strife is like opening a floodgate. Once the gate is opened it is impossible to hold back the water. The same is true concerning conflicts. Once a conflict is started it is almost impossible to keep it from getting out of hand. How many people are in the grave or in prison, how many homes have been torn asunder, how many friendships have been torn apart because of conflict that got out of hand?

Those who are wise will do all they can to avoid strife. When it is impossible to avoid, they will do all they can to solve the problem or to prevent it from getting out of control. That is precisely what Abraham did when there was strife between his herdsmen and Lot's herdsmen. He actually went out of his way to resolve the dispute. He was not trying to solve the problem for his pleasure, convenience, or benefit. He kept Lot's best interest at heart. He was willing to lose to bring about peace. Years later our Lord said, "Blessed are the peacemakers: for they shall be called the children of God." (Matthew 5:9) Do you promote peace, or do you encourage strife? God has a place reserved for each one of us. Will you be satisfied with the place that is reserved for you?

80

*"And, behold, the word of the LORD **came** unto him, saying, This shall not be thine heir; but he that shall come forth out of thine own bowels shall be thine heir." (Genesis 15:4a)*

Have you recently thought about how important the Word of God is, and how empty and confusing life would be if there were no Word from the Lord to guide and encourage us along the way? The thought of having no Word from the Lord is exceptionally terrifying. Even more petrifying is that there are so many people today who are living as if there is no word from the Lord. People are doing what is right in their own sight. They make up the rules as they go. The Word of God has nothing to offer them because as far as they are concerned it is antiquated and irrelevant. They embrace the latest trends rather than the Word of God. When they are concerned about how their day is going to turn out, they read the horoscope. When they need encouragement, they read self-help books. Instead of turning to the church, they join social clubs. Instead of leaning on God, they lean on themselves, their friends, bank account, and many other things that seem to take the place of God. The Word of God, which is their guide and the only book that can satisfy the soul and lead to life, is often neglected. No wonder the home, the church, and the community are falling apart. People are acting as if there is no Word from the Lord. As long as people act that way, we cannot expect things to get any better. Without the Word of God, they have no guide and no hope.

It was the Word of the Lord God that gave Abraham hope amid despair. God had blessed Abraham and Sarah in so many ways. They had everything money could buy. But there was one thing lacking in

159

their lives. They were childless and reaching the age when childbearing would be impossible. Being childless drove Abraham to despair. This meant that the heir of his estate would be the steward of his household, Eliezer of Damascus. He had put his trust in God, but it seemed as if God were going back on His Word. God had promised him a child, but there was no child in sight. God was moving too slowly, and this was playing havoc upon Abraham's thoughts and heart. Abraham was about to give up on God.

When Abraham was on the verge of giving up, the word of the Lord came to him to reassure him. God informed Abraham that Eliezer would not be his heir, but a son would come from his own body to be his heir. God's Word is sure. God always keeps His Word.

Perhaps you have been overwhelmed by the vicissitudes of life. It seems as if God has gone back on His Word, and you are ready to throw in the towel. What you need more than anything is a Word from God for your situation. The truth is that there is a Word from the Lord just for you. So, fine-tune your spiritual ears and hear the Word of the Lord. Let me remind you that to hear His Word, you must turn to his Word. Are you ready to pick up His Word and listen? Are you prepared to hear His preached Word?

81

"But ye shall receive power, after that the Holy Ghost is come upon you: and ye shall be witnesses unto me both in Jerusalem, and in all Judaea, and in Samaria, and unto the uttermost part of the earth." (Acts 1:8)

Some feel a sense of uneasiness when the subject of power comes up. They understand that power can be a blessing in the right hands. On the other hand, they also know that power can be a curse in the wrong hands. Power tends to corrupt and is often found in the wrong hands. It really seems that those who are morally corrupt and willing to promote the agenda of this world have the most power. The more power one has, the more immorality he engages in and supports. Power is often used to tyrannize and take advantage of others. The greater the power, the greater the abuse, and it is the misuse of power that keeps a smile on Satan's face. I can imagine that his smile is more significant than ever when Christians abuse their power. If it were not for the grace and mercy of God, there would be no end to the maltreatment and subjugation by the power in one's hand.

There are many forms of power: the power of wealth, the power of an office, the power of information, the power of charisma, the power of skill, the power of influence, the power of physical strength, the power of military resources, etc. We also think of power in such terms as a powerful argument, a powerful book, a powerful thought, a powerful computer, or a powerful sermon. Power is the ability to accomplish an end. Let me add here that all power comes from God and belongs to God.

Luke informs us that before Jesus ascended to heaven, He promised His disciples that they would receive power when the Holy Ghost came upon them, and they would become His witnesses throughout the world. I am sure that this power includes courage, boldness, confidence, discernment, faith, ability, and to some degree, physical strength, without which it would be impossible to be competent witnesses of Jesus Christ. It is a mistake to try to witness in our power. Witnessing is not about what we can do for God, but about sharing with others what God has done and is doing for us.

God has given us exactly what we need to share the Good News of Jesus Christ with those who are in our inner and outer circle. How are you contributing to the ever-expanding testimony of God's mercy and grace?

82

*"Then the same day at evening, being the first **day** of the week,*
when the doors were shut where the disciples were assembled for
fear of the Jews, came Jesus and stood in the midst, and saith unto
*them, Peace **be** unto you." (John 20:19)*

Sunday is an incredibly extraordinary day. What makes it so special is that it is the first day of the week, the Christian Sabbath, a day of worship. The Christian Sabbath is not the seventh day of the week, but the first day of the week. It is referred to as the Lord's Day, a day when Christians come together and celebrate the Resurrection. The biblical Sabbath is the seventh day, which is Saturday. It commemorates God's rest after He completed His work of creation.

Those of us who follow Jesus know that every day is a special day. Every day is unique because it is a day that the Lord has made; therefore, we are going to do our best to rejoice in it and use our time wisely by making the best of it. Sunday, however, is the one day of the week that we dedicate a portion of our time to worship God. It is no secret that all of our time is in the hands of God. For that reason, we are obligated to give God a portion of the time He has blessed us with to worship Him.

We know that any time is a good time to worship God. If we feel like worshipping God at home, on the job, going down the street, or in the shower, we can go ahead and worship Him. God is always pleased when we worship Him and will accept our worship whenever we offer it to Him. Worship is not just for Sunday. It takes place whenever we experience God's presence and respond to His presence thankfully and lovingly. Worship takes place when we pour out our hearts to God.

Worship occurs whenever we acknowledge that we cannot make it on our own and that we desperately need God.

We can worship God anywhere and at any time; that is a fact. But Sunday is that special day that has been set aside for worship. That is the day that we plan to worship God. We usually arise on Sunday morning with our mind stayed on Jesus. We don't get in a hurry, but on the other hand we are in a hurry and excited about entering God's house for worship. However, we just don't rush into God's house any kind of way. We prayerfully and carefully prepare ourselves to worship God. We look forward to and are excited about meeting God in His house for worship. That is what Sunday is all about. It is about encountering God in worship. When we worship God, not only is He blessed. We too are blessed as we receive courage, peace, hope, and spiritual healing.

Everyone does not feel the same way we feel about Sunday. Some see Sunday as just another day. They don't make any kind of preparation for worship. Sunday is a day where they kick back and take it easy and rest. Rather than taking time to prepare for worship they prepare for the week ahead. Which group do you belong to? Is Sunday a day of planned worship or a day where you plan for the rest of the week?

83

*"And Isaac trembled very exceedingly, and said, Who? where **is** he that hath taken venison, and brought **it** me, and I have eaten of all before thou camest, and have blessed him? yea, **and** he shall be blessed." (Genesis 27:33)*

Imagine for a moment that you are dreaming. In your dream God came to you and said to you, "Ask of me anything you want." What would you ask for? Whatever you ask for will reveal what you are all about. Would you ask for silver and gold? Would you ask for fame and fortune? Would you ask for good health and longevity? Would you ask for a miracle drug that would cure cancer? What would you ask God for?

I know of such a man that had such a dream. His name was Solomon. After he had been made king, God came to him in a dream and said: "Ask what I shall give thee." (1 Kings 3:5b) Solomon knew of the seriousness of this request of God; therefore, he did not immediately request what he wanted. First, he began to talk about how thankful he was that God had been good to his father, David, and for allowing him to continue David's dynasty. Solomon knew that his kingship had nothing to do with merit but had everything to do with God's mercy and grace. He also talked about his helplessness and inadequacy for the awesome task given to him. He knew what was expected of him as king, but he had no idea of how to implement his duties and perform his task as king. He had no idea what he should do. He was like a lost ball in high weeds.

After Solomon expressed his gratitude and his sense of helplessness, he expressed what he wanted the Lord to give him. Perhaps not many people would make such a request as Solomon did. He requested a discerning heart so that he might govern God's people and discern between good and evil, right and wrong. Without this wisdom of discernment, he knew that he would not be able to be an effective king.

Isaac needed such wisdom of discernment as he blessed Jacob instead of Esau. He knew in his heart that something was not right. He even said: "The voice is the voice of Jacob, but the hands are the hands of Esau." (Genesis 27:22) He knew something was wrong. He knew that Jacob's voice and Esau's hands did not go together. But because he was determined to bless Esau, he mistakenly blessed Jacob. The blessing could not be reversed. When Isaac found out what he had done, he trembled very exceedingly and said, "Who? where *is* he that hath taken venison, and brought *it* me, and I have eaten of all before thou camest, and have blessed him? yea, *and* he shall be blessed." (Genesis 27:33) In other words, Isaac was letting Esau know that he could not reverse the blessing.

The lack of spiritual discernment will cause us to do some things that will make us tremble and wish we could go back and change things. But that is impossible. When we are governed by our conscience rather than spiritual discernment, it is difficult to distinguish between good and bad, right and wrong, truth and falsehood, and righteousness and evil.

84

"I came not to call the righteous, but sinners to repentance."
(Luke 5:32)

It is a fact that God walked among us in human form. He did not just appear to be in human form, as some have claimed. He visited us in real human form. God became man and walked among us. How He can be God and man at the same time is one of the greatest mysteries of all times. I say one of the greatest mysteries because his birth and vicarious death are also great mysteries. No one can explain these miraculous events, even though much has been said about these events and people will continue to talk about them. I am glad that it is not required of us to explain these particular miracles concerning the Lord God. If that were the case, all of us would be in serious trouble. The only thing the Lord God requires of us is to believe. The sad news is that many have chosen not to believe. They have no idea of the ultimate dangerous eternal predicament in which they have placed themselves. Thank God that we believe.

God walked among us in the person of Jesus of Nazareth. While he walked among us, He performed many miracles. People were impressed by His miracles and glorified God. (Matthew 15:31) Even though Jesus performed many miracles, that was not His primary purpose for coming into the world. His goal transcended that of being just a miracle worker. If you want to understand the meaning of Jesus' advent, you need to take a good look at the kind of people he hung out with.

Jesus hung out with the kind of people the religious leaders had nothing to do with—tax collectors and sinners (v. 21). Not only did Jesus befriend such people, but he also dined with them. Eating and drinking with them denoted that Jesus identified himself with them. He was one with those whom the religious leaders rejected. The religious leaders complained about Jesus eating and drinking with such people. Instead of complaining, they should have taken a place at the table as repenting sinners before Christ, but they remained blind to their condition before God.

It is because Jesus associated with those who were not socially accepted that we discover his purpose for coming into the world. In response to the religious leaders' complaints, Jesus reveals his mission. He had "not come to call the righteous, but sinners to repentance." Those who are well do not need a doctor. Sick people do. Jesus was and still is the spiritual doctor. At this particular point, Jesus' emphasis was not on the righteous but the sinner. His purpose for coming into the world was to make contact with those in need of repentance, those in need of a change of heart, and those in need of a change of life.

Jesus was accused of spending time with the wrong people. Can anyone criticize you or your church for befriending the wrong people? If not, make it your business to follow God's guidance into the lives of those who need to experience His grace and mercy. Could anyone criticize you or your church for hanging out with the wrong crowd? If not, make it a matter of prayer for God to move you into the lives of one or two people who need to experience His grace and mercy.

85

"Go and tell David my servant, Thus saith the LORD, Thou shalt not build me an house to dwell in." (1 Chronicles 17:4)

God made us with two ears and one mouth which could suggest that God intended for us to do far more listening than talking. While that may be, I think that many of us seem to do more talking than listening. The reasons for that are: (1) some people seem to believe that they have all the answers; therefore, it is difficult for them to be quiet, (2) others seem to love to hear themselves talk, because they think they have rhetoric down pat, (3) some think more highly of themselves than they ought to because of their superb vocabulary, and they love showing off, and (4) for some, it is much easier to talk than to listen. The very reason that so many of us are always getting in some kind of trouble is due to a lack of listening. We talk too much. We need to take the time to listen. Relationships have been torn asunder because someone talked too much. Talkers never take the time to listen. They don't listen to others, and they don't listen to God. Listening is the key to good relationships. It is a sign of caring, and people love to be around those who care.

There is no question about it: effective talking or speaking requires skill. Listening to others or listening to God also requires skill. Listening is crucial for discovering God's will regarding specific issues and Christian living. Listening will enable us to avoid certain pitfalls in life, and is the key to walking with God. James reminds us that we should be "swift to hear, slow to speak." (James 1:19b) We ought to listen to others, but most of all we need to listen to God. That is precisely what the prophet Nathan did.

Let me say that at first Nathan listened to David as he expressed his desire to build God a house. He thought that God would be pleased with David's desire because it was a good desire. Let me remind you that because a thing is good does not mean that it is God's will for you to do it. Nathan was reminded of that fact later on that night when everything was quiet. When he was not bothered by the hustle and bustle of the day, Nathan heard the voice of God. God is constantly speaking to us, but there are times when we cannot discern His voice because of the many voices that speak to us. It was in the stillness of the night when Nathan clearly heard the voice of God informing him that David was not the one who would build Him a temple. After hearing from God, it was Nathan's responsibility to inform David of God's will.

God is still speaking today through various ways, but He speaks mostly through His Word. Are you listening to God as He speaks through His Word? It does you no good to listen to the Word of God and then go your own way. Nathan heard God's Word and became a doer of God's Word. That is the goal of listening to God's Word. You can measure the effectiveness of hearing God's Word by the effect it has on your daily life. Do you use God's Word as a guide for daily living? God would have it no other way.

86

"And when they had prayed, the place was shaken where they were assembled together; and they were all filled with the Holy Ghost, and they spake the word of God with boldness." (Acts 4:31)

Prayer is extremely important in the Christian life. Prayer was given to us by God, our heavenly Father. He did not give us the gift of prayer for His good, but for our good. He was not lonely or needing us to talk to Him every once in a while. God does not need us to talk to Him to make His day. He is surrounded with many heavenly hosts of all kinds that perpetually praise His holy name. So, when God gave us the gift of prayer, and what a gift it is, He had our best interest in mind. He was thinking of us. He knew that it would be challenging for us to make it through life without communicating with Him. It is God who holds our life in His hands. He not only holds our life in His hands, but He has the master plan for our life. Therefore, it just makes good sense to talk and to stay in contact with Him who holds the master plan. We should be forever thankful to God for giving us the gift of prayer. I speak of prayer as a gift, not in the sense of an exceptional talent that God gives specific individuals, but as an opportunity that God gives all of us to communicate with Him. Even the repenting sinner has this opportunity.

What part does prayer play in your life? Are you taking advantage of this grand opportunity to commune with God? Perhaps you are like so many who don't call on God until they encounter a situation that overwhelms them. I was teaching about the importance of prayer in Bible study when a particular individual (who was a great worker in the church) sent shock waves through my body when she confessed that the only time she prays is when she needs something from God or is in serious trouble. Another person admitted that he doesn't talk to God about the little issues in his life because he thinks God is not concerned about them and expects us to handle them. He went on to say that he only talks to God about the significant issues. It is sad to say, but they are not the only persons that feel that way about prayer. So many people make the mistake of endeavoring to go through life leaning and depending on their wisdom and strength. Prayer is not something they engage in daily. Prayer is reserved for those tough issues. This is not the way God intended for it to be. Prayer should play a significant part in our lives rather than a minor role.

Through His Word, God encourages us to pray without ceasing. (1 Thessalonians 5:17) Prayer ought to be a part of our very being. We should perpetually talk to God about everything that is going on in our lives and in the lives of others. God wants us to bring everything to Him in prayer, because He cares about us and everything that is going on in our lives. No matter is too small or too large to take to God in prayer. "Be careful for nothing; but in every thing by prayer and supplication with thanksgiving let your requests be made known unto God." (Philippians 4:6) Let me remind you that prayer is not a waste of our time or God's time. When we pray, something will happen. That is a fact.

God has put prayer within our reach. Have you reached out and taken a permanent hold on prayer? Have you made prayer a very constant part of your life? If not, what are you waiting for? God is waiting for you to commune with Him. Don't keep God waiting.

87

*"And Jacob awaked out of his sleep, and he said, Surely the LORD is in this place; and I knew **it** not." (Genesis 28:16)*

How often do we go about from day to day without recognizing the presence of God in our lives? At times we are so busy doing our thing that we don't pay any attention to God's presence. We don't even think about His presence being so near to us. If the truth is told, there are moments when His presence seems to be very far from us rather than close to us. Such times are not the best times for those of us who love the Lord. Such instances cause us to lose our focus and take matters into our own hands, which denotes that we are on our own. On our own is the worst position we can ever be in. To take matters into our hands and act as if there is no God is foolish and dangerous. God wants us to recognize and embrace His presence and direct our lives accordingly.

No matter what is going on in our lives, God is always present. He is present in the good times as well as the bad. He is present when we are busy and when we are not. God is always revealing Himself to us in some way. Sometimes God reveals Himself in many small ways. At other times, He reveals Himself in some spectacular way. God is never absent in our lives. He is always present, and I thank God for that. The thought that God is not near to us is too much for me to even think about. I cannot imagine going through life without the presence of God. I know that God is transcendent, but I also know that He is very close. Knowing that God is with us makes all the difference in the world. His presence can change the way we see life, change the direction of our lives, and cause us to make a serious commitment to Him. His presence is the most fabulous presence this world has ever known.

Jacob discovered that for himself. He was on the run from the wrath of his brother Esau. Perhaps he was filled with guilt, fear, and shame. He came to a certain place—Bethel, which means the house of God. As he slept, God revealed Himself to Jacob. Perhaps for the first time in his life, he sensed the presence of God. When he awoke, he cried out, "Surely the LORD is in this place; and I knew *it* not." (Genesis 28:16)

It was the discovery of God's presence that changed Jacob's life. God's presence brought reassurance in a time of doubt, security in a time of insecurity, guidance in a time of misguidance, and comfort in a time of discomfort. The discovery of the presence of God led Jacob to commit his life to God. God revealed Himself to Jacob in a time of great need. This revelation of Himself had nothing to do with merit. It had everything to do with grace. That is the kind of God we serve. He cares about us and is perpetually making His presence known to us because He wants to guide us through life.

God is making His presence known to you at this very moment. He is doing so because He cares for you, wants to assist you, and wants to guide you through life. How will you respond to God's presence? Will you ignore His presence and go your own way, or will you lean and depend upon His presence for the rest of your life?

88

*"Now why dost thou cry out aloud? **is there** no king in thee? is thy counsellor perished? for pangs have taken thee as a woman in travail." (Micah 4:9)*

There is no such thing as a trouble-free life. There may be periods of serenity and security, but sooner or later people will succumb to disappointments and dilemmas. That is just the way life is. Even when things are going well, there will be some kind of catch-22 hanging around for you to deal with. Even a rose garden, as beautiful as it is, has thorns. Trouble and disappointment are a part of the world we live in. That is an undisputed fact.

The million-dollar question is: How are people dealing with their disenchantments and tribulations? Too many people are going about it the wrong way. They complain to everyone they see about how bad things are for them. Complaining has never helped anyone. The truth is that complaining often makes things worse because it causes one to focus on the problem rather than a solution. Some turn to alcohol, drugs, and partying, which in the long run create a greater giant for them to deal with. Many read all kinds of books trying to find a solution to their problems. Not too long ago, a young lady who was not satisfied with her marriage asked me about a good book on marriage so she could give it to her husband to read.

The story has gone viral about a particular pastor who is going to take a sabbatical from his church because he is entirely burned out. He brought out that he has even gotten out of touch with God. He feels that what he needs is rest and then he will be able to get himself together. All of us need to take time to rest. Even Jesus took the time to steal away

175

and rest from time to time. However, I feel that this pastor is looking in the wrong place to solve his problem. He is leaning toward a physical or carnal solution to solve a spiritual problem, which might lead to a false sense of relief, which could lead to a more significant problem. Like everybody else, this man of God is looking in the wrong place to solve his problem. The sad news is that his action will cause many to look in the same direction to solve their problems.

Micah would have us to know that as long as we look in the wrong places for help, we will continue to experience pain and disappointment, just like a woman in travail. All the things that we have depended upon to bring peace, security, and satisfaction will let us down and will ultimately lead to greater agony. As long as we keep acting as if there is no God, the greater the pain and frustration will be. It is always dangerous to use carnal means to solve carnal problems. It is much more dangerous to use carnal means to solve spiritual problems. No wonder we are complaining and falling apart. It is God's will that we stop looking at things that will let us down and start looking to Him. Are you looking to God or are you looking to other means? God is our help in times of trouble.

89

"Behold, I stand at the door, and knock: if any man hear my voice,
and open the door, I will come in to him, and will sup with him,
and he with me." (Revelation 3:20)

There is no doubt among believers that Jesus is the Savior of the world. However, people have different views of Jesus. Some see Him as the greatest man that ever lived. Others see Him as a great miracle worker. Several people see Him as a great prophet. Some see Him as just another man. I talked to one individual who claims that Jesus was "no more than a fable to get people to live a better life."

The Bible depicts Him as the King of Kings, the Great Physician, the lover of children and all people, the friend of sinners, the fulfillment of prophecy, the light and salt of the earth, liberator of the oppressed, the Savior of the world, etc. The more we read the Bible, the more we discover about Jesus. He is presented in many different ways, and all of them are true. Jesus means many things to many different people. What is your favorite picture of Jesus depicted in the Bible?

This particular text represents one of the most poignant pictures of Jesus in the Bible. It describes Jesus as loving us so much that He actually goes out of His way to make contact with undeserving and ungrateful sinners. The opposite should be true. We should be going out of our way to make contact with Him and maintain it because we need Him. Regardless, it is always Jesus who makes the first move to meet our greatest need which is to prepare us for eternity while living on this side. If He waited for us to come to Him, it might never happen. We tend to go in the opposite direction, away from God rather than toward Him. That is the very reason He comes to us. That tells us a lot about God. He loves us more than we love ourselves. He loves us so much that He wants us to spend eternity in His presence. He always has our best interests at heart. He is not only concerned about the future, but He is also concerned about the present. Right now, He wants to come into our lives and bless us. He is eager to make His presence known not only to sinners but to those who have professed Him. He wants to make Himself known in every area of our lives. Have you shut Him out of your life through irreverence, negligence, absent-mindedness, lack of faith, or disobedience?

90

*"And if I go and prepare a place for you, I will come again, and
receive you unto myself; that where I am, **there** ye may be also."*
(John 14:3)

I firmly believe in the Bible. I believe that the Bible is the Word of God.
I am convinced in my heart that everything from Genesis to Revelation
is God-breathed. "All scripture *is* given by inspiration of God, and *is*
profitable for doctrine, for reproof, for correction, for instruction in
righteousness." (2 Timothy 3:16) The entire Bible is inspired, including
those Scriptures that do not speak well of Jesus the Son of God. The
Bible teaches us how we are to live as children of the most-high God. It
corrects us when we are wrong and puts us on a path of righteousness.
The Bible teaches us all that we need to know about God, humanity,
and sin. I believe that the Bible speaks to all of our issues directly or
indirectly. Therefore, if we have any questions about any of the things
that are trending today, we should allow God's Word to be our guide.
One of the problems we are faced with today is that some think that
God is bigger than the Bible; therefore, they look to other sources for
answers which causes them to accept what is popular rather than what
is right according to God's Word. I agree that God is much larger than
the Bible, but the Bible is all that we have, and we should stay with the
Word of God.

The words of the Bible give us hope regarding spending eternity
with God. We embrace these words with all of our hearts because they
are the Word of God. The good news is that we can trust the Word of God
because there is no record where He has ever gone back on His Word.
If God said it, we can take it to the bank. It would do us well not only

to believe this particular passage but also to memorize this passage and allow these Words of our Lord to dwell in us richly, instructing us, comforting us, and encouraging us.

No matter what is going on in our lives, we have something to look forward to. Christ has promised us that He will come again and take us to Himself so that we will be with Him forever. The only promise that would be greater than this promise is the promise that He is coming back today. In that light, let us live as if He is coming back today. Let us live today with a new destiny in view. Are you living with heaven in your view?

91

*"And he said, My presence shall go **with thee**,*
and I will give thee rest." (Exodus 33:14)

Our greatest need is to have God come along beside us and remain with us. It is a great blessing to be able to walk and talk with God daily. I cannot imagine how difficult life would be if God refused to come along beside us. I don't know what I would do without God in my life. I am convinced beyond any shadow of a doubt that without Him I could do nothing. Without Him I would be like a lost ball in high weeds. I really need God. He is my greatest need.

As we journey from earth to heaven, there will be times in which all of us will say, "Lord we have no one but you." It is at that juncture that we come to know for a fact that God is our greatest need. We need Him more than anything. We need Him more than silver and gold. We need Him more than friends and fame. It is when we respond to Him and embrace Him that He will respond to us and embrace us.

There are many today who want the benefits of God rather than God Himself. They want the blessings more than they want the one who blesses. Some put more emphasis on the blessing than on the one who blesses. Perhaps that is the reason why the prosperity movement is so popular among many young people. The truth is that God is able to bless them regardless of the church they attend. The fact that they must never lose sight of is that God Himself is the greatest gift of all. There is nothing like being in a real and vital relationship with God.

Knowing God is better than anything else. How wonderful it is to have God come along beside us to walk and talk with us. His presence makes all the difference in the world. God's presence is worth more than any blessings anyone can ever receive. Only the presence of God can fill the void in people's lives. Do you want the blessings without a personal relationship with God?

God gave Moses a great promise, which was the promise of His very own presence and rest: "I will go with you and give you rest." (Exodus 33:14) If God did not go with them, Moses did not want to continue the journey. This shows the great priority Moses put on the presence of God, a priority seldom seen at any age. Does God's presence take precedence in your life? Are you experiencing the benefits of God's presence?

92

"For the LORD, the God of Israel, saith that he hateth putting away."
(Malachi 2:16)

The words "hateth putting away" refer to divorce. God hates divorce. This world would be better off if its people felt the same way about it. Divorce is playing havoc with this country, and nobody seems to be doing anything about it. The family structure is being torn asunder because of divorce. When the family structure begins to crumble and fall, so does everything else in the community. Divorce has long-term, devastating effects upon children, which include drug abuse, a rebellious spirit, trust problems, depression, and disrespect for the family structure.

Divorce is no respecter of persons. It will overtake any married couple who fail to take their marriage vows seriously and are not willing to fight for their marriage. There is no such thing as divorce insurance that guarantees that a marriage will not end in divorce. Many who are going through the agony of divorce never thought that it would happen to them.

Joyful, well-built marriages are absolutely possible, but it takes work—a perpetual effort. When two people enter into a marital relationship, trouble and difficulties are inevitable at times. They must not allow those adverse moments to control them. Even though they cannot control the moments, they must be able to control their response in those moments. It is not how much trouble they face but how they face the trouble that makes a real difference.

The problem with most of our marriages is that sacrifice has succumbed to selfishness. If we want to have a marriage that pleases

God, then our marriage must reflect His sacrificial love. We have got to keep God at the center of our marriages. The Bible teaches us that there is only one God and that we should not put any other god before Him. In that light, we must remember never to allow our spouse to become our god. If we implement that truth, our marriage will more likely be healthy.

The church should be involved in a ministry of divorce prevention. Despite such a ministry, divorces will occur; therefore, we need to make sure that we also have some type of ministry in place to offer comfort and hope for those who are experiencing or have experienced the agony of divorce. In compassion, we need to pray for, support, and encourage those who have undergone this traumatic experience.

What are you doing to make your marriage pleasing in the sight of God? Are you striving to make the best of your marriage? Do you understand that there is no such thing as a problem-free marriage? Are you willing to acknowledge these problems and move forward to make the best of your marriage? Do you understand that certain things must be avoided at all cost because they will lead to serious trouble? Are you seeking solutions to the existing problems?

93

"In the beginning God created the heaven and the earth."
(Genesis 1:1)

The creation of the world is a fascinating subject. The thing that amazes me about this subject is that some speak of creation and completely leave God out of the equation. I cannot wrap my mind around how anyone can talk about creation and leave God out. To leave God out of the creation story is to have no story at all. It is to have nothing at all. Without God, there is absolutely nothing. Nothing from nothing leaves nothing. Creation suggests that there is a creator. This Creator is God. No matter what theory you come up with regarding creation, it does not make any sense if you leave God out. Nothing makes sense without God. The only thing that makes sense regarding creation is, "In the beginning God created." If you are convinced that the world came about through evolution, I will not argue with you as long as you say, "In the beginning God..." It was God and God alone who started the process. If you are convinced that the world came about through a big bang, I have no problem with that as long as you say, "In the beginning God..." It was God who caused the big bang. Nothing happens without God. That is a fact. Even if you don't believe in God, you must agree that something or somebody is behind creation, and whatever you call that something or someone, He is still God.

The creation story tells us something about God. The first thing it suggests is that there is none like Him. If there just happen to be other gods, which is not the case, they cannot compare to Him. He is in a class all by Himself. Second, it suggests that God is all powerful. To be able to create something out of nothing declares that God is all powerful. To make something out of existing material is no big thing. But to create something out of nothing is unheard of. Such a feat can only be associated with an all-powerful God. Third, the creation story reminds us that God had a plan for His creation. He did not create the world and all that is within it, including humanity, just to be doing something or because He was lonely. He had many heavenly creatures to keep Him company. He created because He had a plan, which reminds us of His sovereignty. God is able to implement His plan and is doing so. God is in complete control. Even when it looks as if things are out of control, even when it seems as if someone else is in charge, God is still in control, and He knows exactly what He is doing.

This world didn't just happen to come into existence. God brought it into being. None of us are here by accident, even if our birth was not planned or we were born out of wedlock. God could have prevented our birth from taking place, but He did not. He formed us while we were in our mother's womb. We were fearfully and wonderfully made by God. (Psalm 139:14) God knew precisely what He was doing when He made us, and He is satisfied with what He created and loves us to the utmost. So, let us be satisfied with the way we look, with the skin we are in, with the gift or gifts He has endowed to us, and be determined to praise Him throughout this year and the years to come despite the trials and tribulations that confront us. Let us give the God of creation all the praise and glory, for He deserves it. Are you willing to do just that for the rest of your life?

94

*"So God created man in his **own** image, in the image of God created he him; male and female created he them." (Genesis 1:27)*

It is an honor to be created in the image of God. It is the image of God that distinguishes us from the rest of creation. It is this image that provides us with dignity and honor. God made us from dust, which has no value at all. People spend a lot of time, energy, and money to get rid of dust from their homes, cars, and offices. Dust can be very annoying. No one likes to be around a lot of dust. It can cause all kinds of allergies. While that may be, God chose to make us out of useless and valueless dust. We were taken from dust and will return to dust. Dirt has some value, but dust has no value at all. People will buy dirt, but I have never heard of anyone buying dust. God scooped up a little dust, and with His own hands formed man and breathed into his nostrils, and man became a living soul which was created in the image of God. Humanity is the highlight of God's creation. God is the most powerful, authoritative being in all creation, and man is the only created being that possesses the image of God.

Too often, we take being made in the image of God for granted. Time and again, we fail to act as if we were made in the image of God. Again and again, we fail to appreciate that we were made in the image of God. Instead of trying to become more like God, too often we strive to become more like the world. This is not always a deliberate act. It has become a part of our culture. We do it without thinking about what we are doing. It is time for us to stop taking being made in the image of God for granted. We need to give serious thought to being made in the image of God. All of us possess the image of God. It is time for us to start acting like it. God did not just throw us together as if we were an afterthought. He intentionally used His own hands and purposely created us in His own image. God had something special in mind when He created humankind. "What is man, that thou art mindful of him? and the son of man, that thou visitest him? For thou hast made him a little lower than the angels, and hast crowned him with glory and honour. Thou madest him to have dominion over the works of thy hands; thou hast put all *things* under his feet." (Psalm 8:4–6)

To be made in the image of God is one of God's greatest gifts to humankind. It is time for us to stop taking God's gift for granted and start living as if we were made in His image. What about you? Does your daily life reflect that you were made in His image?

95

"If ye love me, keep my commandments."
(John 14:15)

Talk is cheap. We can make our mouth say anything. We can say anything we want to say without any sense of commitment. We can talk about love all day long. We can talk about how much we love Jesus all day long. Talking about loving Jesus is one thing, but loving Him is something altogether different. Talk is easy, but loving Jesus is about real commitment and sacrifice. True love always takes us out of our way. It is not always convenient to love someone. Certain people make it hard for us to love them, but real love has a way of hanging in there with difficult people.

Do you think that it was convenient for Jesus to love us? When we think about all He went through to show us just how much He loves us, we know that it was not convenient for Him to love us. He had to give up His equality with God to save us. He had to leave His heavenly home and become one of us to save us. That is just how much He loved us. He just didn't talk about how much He loved us. He took the proper action to prove His love for us. Notice that I did not say that Jesus took action to prove His love for us, but I said that He took the *proper* action to prove His love. That is very important because only the appropriate action, not just any action, brings out our love for Jesus and others.

Some actions will definitely prove the very opposite of our love. That was not the case with Jesus. Everything He did proved that He loved us. He took the worst that man threw at Him, even death on a rugged cross, to prove His love for us. He never complained about suffering at the hands of man; in fact, He counted it all joy. That is the kind of Lord

He is. Now, when we think about when He did all of this for us (while we were yet sinners), all we can do is bow our heads, stroke our breasts, think of his grace, and cry out, "Greater love hath no man than this, that a man lay down his life for his friends." (John 15:13) Love is not cheap. It never has been or ever will be. Jesus' love for us cost Him His life.

Too often, people think of the word love as a noun rather than a verb. Love is not passive; love is active. It is time for us to stop talking about how much we love Jesus and take the proper action to prove our love for Jesus. Love is not something that we talk about, but it is something that we do. Jesus showed us just how much He loves us. What are you doing to show the world and Jesus just how much you love Him? "If ye love me, keep my commandments." (John 14:15)

96

"Take heed to yourselves: If thy brother trespass against thee, rebuke him; and if he repent, forgive him." (Luke 17:3)

It would be a good thing if all of us were perfect. The truth is that there is no such thing as perfection on this side of eternity. All of us fall short. All of us make mistakes. No one is exempted. It makes no difference where you come from, how much you have, what color your skin is, or your status in life. We all fall short. We all mistreat others at times. We abuse our family members, our neighborhood, those we work with, people in the church, and those who are different from us. People all over the world need to implement the teaching of our Lord regarding forgiveness.

It is impossible to go through this life without experiencing some form of mistreatment. Someone will take advantage of us along the way. Not only will someone take advantage of us, but we will also take advantage of others. Sometimes it will be deliberately; at other times it will not be intentional, but it will happen. Those who are supposed to keep our best interest at heart will, at times, mistreat us. Parents abuse their children. Children mistreat their parents. Some churches misuse their pastors. Some pastors take advantage of the church. Some spouses mishandle their spouse. They treat their spouse as if he/she is nothing but a piece of property. There are thousands and thousands of people who have been seriously scarred because of the pain others have inflicted upon them.

The question is how we will deal with those who mistreat us. The natural thing to do is to get even. We have been taught not to let people run over us. Those who do so are considered weak, and we do not like the idea of being weak. We can also try to avoid those who hurt us, but that is not always possible because we sometimes work with them and live with them. On the other hand, it would do us much good to seriously consider how our Lord wants us to handle the situation.

Seriously considering what the Lord wants us to do is not always in agreement with us, but it is always in our best interest and the best interest of others. Our Lord's will is that we forgive those who hurt us in some way. We are obligated to do so. This is not a suggestion from our Lord. It is a requirement that we somehow embrace a forgiving spirit in dealing with the injuries that are inflicted upon us by others.

Forgiveness is not always easy. The greater the pain, the harder it is to forgive. Forgiveness will not automatically happen. We must strive to embrace such a spirit. Sometimes it is a long and difficult process, but all things are possible with God. Are you striving to embrace such a spirit, which pleases our Lord? Are you holding a grudge in your heart? To harbor grudges is to be like the world. To forgive is to be like Christ.

97

"In whom also after that ye believed, ye were sealed with that holy Spirit of promise, Which is the earnest of our inheritance until the redemption of the purchased possession, unto the praise of his glory." (Ephesians 1:13b-14)

Promises, promises, promises, we all know what a promise is. A promise is a guarantee that something will certainly happen or be done. Broken promises have caused many of us not to put much stock in a promise. They seem to be no more than words that are void of meaning and purpose. People will make a promise with no intention of keeping it.

Again and again, people have been torn asunder and have given up on people because of broken promises. Often, those who make promises have forgotten about the importance of making their promise a reality. They will promise you anything to win your favor without giving much thought regarding keeping their promise. Many politicians are guilty of breaking their promises. They will make great promises, but when they get into office they act as if they have not promised you anything. The truth is that they frequently do the very opposite of what they promised. Some have even switched parties once they were in office. Can you blame people for not putting much stock in someone's promise? It is surprising when people have enough integrity to keep their word. It should be the other way around. Unfortunately, that is the kind of world we live in—a world that is lacking in morals and integrity.

But there is one in whom we can always trust to keep His promise, and that is God. He is not a man that He should lie. He has never gone back on His Word. His Word means everything to Him. His

Word is impregnated with truth, meaning, and purpose; therefore, we need to be patient and put all of our trust in Him. He will keep His word. If God said it, He would bring it to pass. It is as simple as that. That is just the way God is.

Are you not glad that He is that way? Can you imagine how uncertain life would be if God would say one thing and do something else? Because God never goes back on His promises life has meaning and purpose. But more than that, you are secure now and forever. That is nothing but good news.

God has kept His Word. He has identified us as His very own through the presence of the Holy Spirit in our lives. The Holy Spirit makes us cognizant of the presence and power of God in our lives. He also assures us that we have been adopted into the royal family of God; therefore, we are entitled to His many blessings now and forever. God has kept His promise and given us the promise of the Holy Spirit. What does the fulfillment of this promise mean to you, and how does it affect your daily living?

98

*"And it came to pass, as she spake to Joseph day by day, that he hearkened not unto her, to lie by her, **or** to be with her."*
(Genesis 39:10)

Temptation has been defined as the enticement or invitation to sin, which connotes that some kind of benefit will be attained. Satan has been described as the great tempter. He started with Eve in the Garden of Eden and has been tempting humankind ever since with great success. The only person he was not able to do anything with was Jesus. Regarding Jesus, he absolutely failed. Jesus "was in all points tempted like as we are, yet without sin." (Hebrews 4:15) Satan's plan is to destroy not just some people but everyone through sin. He desires that everyone spends eternity with him in hell. Temptation is the medium through which he implements his plan. Let me remind you that temptation is a tool that belongs to the devil. God has never used this tool and never will. Using such a tool is against the very nature of God. There are times when God allows us to be tested to bring out the best in us, which ultimately honors Him. There is a blessing for everyone who refuses to yield to temptation.

As we journey through life, we have discovered ways and means to avoid many things. We can avoid many dangers by being careful and staying away from certain things, places, and people. We can avoid being put in jail or prison by obeying the law. We can avoid certain sicknesses such as measles, mumps, chickenpox, flu, and pneumonia by getting certain vaccinations for each of these viruses. We can prevent spiritual burnout by staying in touch with God and reading the Bible daily. We can even avoid people who get on our nerves by evading them when it is possible. We can take specific safety measures against diseases, accidents, and illnesses to prevent them. We can evade many disgraceful situations by watching and praying.

There are many things we can avoid by taking the proper action, but there is one thing that we cannot avoid. One thing that every human being has in common is that no one is exempted from temptation. Temptation comes to every person regardless of age, color, or creed.

The good news regarding temptation is that God will not allow us to experience a temptation that is more than we can bear. Not only that, but He will provide a way out the moment the temptation comes. The best thing we can do in that moment is to take God's way of escape, and in doing so we will glorify Him. God is pleased when we follow His plan regarding temptation. Joseph followed God's plan when Potiphar's wife tempted him. How will you handle temptation when it comes? Will you surrender to temptation, or will you flee from it and glorify God in your body?

99

"And when I saw him, I fell at his feet as dead. And he laid his right hand upon me, saying unto me, Fear not; I am the first and the last: I am he that liveth, and was dead; and, behold, I am alive for evermore, Amen; and have the keys of hell and of death."
(Revelation 1:17–18)

We tend at times to be very concerned regarding those elected officials. There are times when we do precisely that which we as followers of the crucified and risen Christ should never do, which is worry. Our Lord informs us not to worry. We should not worry because it never helps to worry and because God cares for us, which suggests that God will take care of us.

However, we still tend to worry at times. We know that elected officials have the authority to do good or to do bad. It seems that many elected officials are more concerned about lining their pockets with wealth and catering to big organizations, the rich, and the middle class than they are about assisting the marginalized. It seems that no one is concerned about the underprivileged. The disadvantaged are often overlooked as if they do not matter at all. Often, they are treated as if they are not human beings. God has established the government for the good of all people, but it doesn't seem to work that way. Those who are concerned about minorities are always outnumbered and cannot do very much to help them. They lack the authority and support to do what they know they should do. Often those of the lower class are embraced by fear and a sense of hopelessness. They know many of the elected officials are working against them.

The Word from heaven today regarding those who are not at the center of attention, influence, or power is, "Fear not; I am the first and the last: I *am* he that liveth, and was dead; and, behold, I am alive for evermore, Amen; and have the keys of hell and of death." (Revelation 1:17-18) Our Lord is the beginning and the end, and all that is in between; therefore, we should not fear. In other words, Jesus is in control of all of life and death. Not even a sparrow falls to the ground without His knowledge. It may seem like the elected officials and the rich and powerful are in control, but the truth is that our Lord is in control. He has always been in control and will always be in control. History has proven again and again that God has always taken care of His people regardless of the mayor, governor, congress, or president. If God has taken care of His people in the past, He is able to do so today and will do so. Are you willing to trust God to see you through, even though many things seem to be against you?

100

"And Abel, he also brought of the firstlings of his flock and of the fat thereof. And the LORD had respect unto Abel and to his offering."
(Genesis 4:4)

Merriam-Webster's Collegiate Dictionary defines respect as "the quality or state of being esteemed." Respect is paramount. Everyone wants to be respected to some degree. Respect is a natural desire. Teenagers, young adults, mature adults, and senior citizens want to be respected. People will even go out of their way to be respected by others. Some people will also engage in things they know are not right to gain the respect of their peers. When people are disrespected, they become angry, develop low self-esteem, and at times will do something foolish to those who disrespect them.

The Bible has much to say about respect. The Bible encourages us to respect our elders (Leviticus 19:32), municipal representatives (Romans 13:7), parents (1 Timothy 3:4), Christian leaders (1 Thessalonians 5:12), and one another (Romans 12:10; Philippians 2:3; 1 Peter 2:17). Those of us who are called by His name should live a life worthy of respect. Time and again, the Bible affirms that God is no respecter of persons. In other words, God does not show partiality; therefore, we are obligated to refrain from disrespecting others.

People spend a lot of time and energy trying to gain the respect of others. Being respected by others gives us a sense of importance. It makes us feel good about ourselves when others respect us. We are encouraged to keep doing what we are doing to keep others respecting us. We even make the mistake of attaining the respect of others as the main goal in life. Seeking the respect of others is not a bad thing in itself, but when seeking the respect of others becomes an end within itself it becomes dangerous. We should be more concerned about seeking the respect of God rather than man. I am not suggesting that we can earn God's respect; we can never do that. We can strive to live a life that is pleasing to Him.

When God sees our sincerity about our living and our worship, He will graciously accept our way of living and worshipping and respect us just as He respected Abel and his offering. Are you seeking God's respect and acceptance, or are you seeking man's respect? To gain God's respect is the highest achievement in life. To gain God's respect, you must respect Him. We respect God when we choose to live and worship on His terms rather than ours.

101

*"And Jacob their father said unto them, Me have ye bereaved **of my children**: Joseph **is** not, and Simeon **is** not, and ye will take Benjamin **away**: all these things are against me."*
(Genesis 42:36)

The way we look at life has everything to do with our attitude about life. It is our attitude that determines how we will deal with the adverse circumstances that occur in our lives. All of us will experience unfavorable circumstances at times. No one is exempted. The first question is not how we will deal with the problem but how we will see the unfortunate situation. The way we perceive the situation is extremely significant. It will determine the action we will take.

If we see the situation as an abysmal one, we will most likely succumb to despair. When that happens, we will allow the circumstance to control us. When we allow that to happen, there is no telling where we will end up. Circumstances will dictate to us what we should do without any sense of grace and mercy. What chance do we have in life without grace and mercy? It is a dangerous thing to be in the powerful grip of unwanted circumstances. To be controlled by an undesirable state of affairs is never in our best interest. Such control will finally lead us to surmise that the thing that is happening to us is a heavy burden which we cannot bear. That is a place that God's children should never go. We should avoid such a place at all costs. Such a place tends to lead us further away from God. The further away we are from God, the heavier our burdens become. The heavier our burdens become, the less likely we will depend upon God. The less we depend upon God, the more likely we will do something foolish and detrimental to our well-being, and the well-being of our family.

If we see our situation, no matter how bad it is or how much it hurts, as one in which God is present, we will always have hope. Knowing that God is in the midst of our dreadful situation removes all fears. Our situation no longer paralyzes us. The appalling circumstance no longer controls us; therefore, we can make a positive response to our situation because we know that God is in control of the situation and is working it out for our good. The things that seem to be working against us are working for us. Things are not what they appear to be. Instead of being a heavy burden, our ill-fated incident becomes a stepping stone that takes us higher and higher. With God, all things are possible. Without Him, a molehill can become a mountain, and all mishaps are against you.

Those who fail to see God in their situation and those who see God in their situation will see two different things. The former will see hopelessness, helplessness, confusion, uncertainty, and stones about their necks. The latter will see hopefulness, understanding, and certainty, but most of all, they will see stepping stones placed there by God to take them over and beyond their troubles. How do you see your troubles? Are they working against you, or are they working in your favor?

102

*"And Enoch walked with God: and he **was** not; for God took him."*
(Genesis 5:24)

The story of Enoch is remarkable. It is impregnated with excitement and joy because Enoch walked with God. Adam hid from God, Cain went from the presence of God, but Enoch walked with God. According to the Biblical record, there were only two men that it was said that they walked with God—Enoch and Noah. Not only does the Bible say that Enoch walked with God, but it also says that He was not. Enoch walked with God, and he was not. In other words, Enoch was not gathered to his people in death as others were. He simply bypassed death and went to heaven. The only other person that avoided death in the Bible is Elijah.

We know that Enoch was not a perfect man. There has only been one perfect man to walk on this side of eternity—the man, Jesus Christ. Enoch had his faults just as we have ours. Something happened to Enoch after the birth of Methuselah. We don't know exactly what happened to him, but we can surmise that it was life-changing. He dedicated his life to God in such a way that he was able to have a closer walk with God which can be described as a walk of total commitment to God, of unbroken communion and fellowship with God. What a walk this was. It occurred after the birth of Methuselah.

Before the birth of Methuselah, Enoch walked as other people walked. He followed the crowd. He did what other people did. For sixty-five years Enoch walked the low road of life, but when Methuselah was born his walk was changed. For three hundred years after that he walked with God and had other children. "And all the days of Methuselah were nine hundred sixty and nine years: and he died." (Genesis 5:27) Enoch lived a long, exciting, and fulfilling life on this earth. The most exciting thing about his life is that he did not die. The record does not say that Enoch died; it says, "And Enoch walked with God: and he was not; for God took him." (Genesis 5:24)

We are challenged to abandon all of our religious activities and engage God with our hearts. Once we engage God with our hearts, we will begin to walk with Him. God has come along beside us so that we can fulfill His desire, and His desire is that we walk with Him. God has made it possible for us to walk with Him. Is God wasting His time? It is God's desire that we walk with Him. Is it our desire to walk with Him? If it is, what are we doing about it?

103

"Then said Jesus unto the twelve, Will ye also go away?"
(John 6:67)

Several years ago, I was fishing with a friend of another hue. It was a good day for fishing, and we were enjoying ourselves. We always enjoyed each other's company. He was much older than I and was dealing with cancer. Fishing was a way to escape the reality of death, at least for a few moments. For a few moments, he could enjoy the present without thinking about his abysmal future. Somehow the words of Paul, "We are confident, *I say*, and willing rather to be absent from the body, and to be present with the Lord," (2 Corinthians 5:8) do not always provide comfort and peace to those who are walking in the very shadow of death and have not made peace with death. They must find some other way to cope with it. Fishing gave my friend a moment of peace as he swiftly accelerated toward death.

As we were fishing on that particular day, he suddenly picked up his fishing tackle and said, "I am going to move downstream; here comes my nephew. He is visiting me this week, and you don't want to be around him. He once was a big Christian, but now he is an atheist." We were catching fish, so I decided to stay. His nephew came up beside me, and the first thing he said was, "Are you a Christian?" I responded, "Yes, I am a Christian." Then he said, "You Christians are the biggest fools I have seen in my life. I used to be a Christian. I taught Sunday School for years, but I finally woke up. I walked away from the church because there is no God, and if He does exist, He is going to send everybody to hell." Before he could continue, I gathered my tackle and went downstream and joined my friend. My friend said as he laughed, "I knew you were not going to stay up there with him. I will be glad when he goes home."

How can anyone come to know Jesus and then walk away? The only answer I can come up with is that this particular person came to know of Jesus. He knew the story of Jesus. He knew of all the facts concerning Jesus. He had head knowledge about Jesus, but he did not know Jesus. There is a vast difference in knowing about Jesus and really knowing Jesus. Knowing about Jesus just might attract one to Jesus for a while, but when the attraction wears off and is no longer fulfilling, people will usually walk away.

That is precisely what the crowd did. They walked away from Jesus to follow Him no more. They were attracted to Jesus without being attached to Him. But on the other hand, the disciples were attracted and attached to Jesus, which led them to see the light. There was nowhere else to go. There is no other way. Jesus, and Jesus only, is the way. What about your relationship with Jesus? Have you discovered that apart from Jesus, there is nowhere else to go?

104

"Take heed unto thyself, and unto the doctrine; continue in them:
for in doing this thou shalt both save thyself, and them
that hear thee." (1 Timothy 4:16)

Several years ago, I was on my way to church one Sunday morning. I had been struggling all week long with this particular sermon. I was not sure about the sermon itself, nor was I sure about God's approval concerning this sermon even though I prayed all through the preparation of the sermon. I did not pray for God's approval of the sermon. I prayed that God would speak and guide me throughout the preparation process. But somehow, I was still not sure that I had the right sermon. Amid my frustration I tried to prepare another sermon more than once, but I kept coming back to that sermon. It seemed like the Lord God would not let me prepare another sermon. Even though I was not sure of the sermon I was working on, God kept bringing me back to that sermon. Finally, I finished that sermon. I left the house on that particular Sunday morning filled with doubt regarding the sermon that I was going to preach.

No sooner had I left the house than I saw this young lady standing on the sidewalk. She was no stranger to me even though I did not know her name. She would often pass by the house and say, "Hey preacher, how are you doing today?" Now and then, she would stop and share with me how others mistreated her with tears in her eyes. She would always conclude her conversation by saying, "It is going to be all right, preacher, because God is on my side. God is going to get those who do me wrong. Ain't that right preacher?" I usually responded by saying, "You got that right."

But on this particular Sunday morning as we greeted each other, she cried out in a loud voice, "Get it right today, preacher." Again and again, she cried out, "Get it right today, preacher. Get it right today, preacher." When I could no longer hear her, I saw her in my rearview mirror standing in the street with both of her hand raised up toward heaven saying, "Get it right today, preacher."

By that time, tears began to run down my face. I had been struggling all week, and I was not sure that I had gotten it right. All the way to church tears flowed from my eyes as I heard her voice in my mind saying, "Get it right today, preacher." As I sat in the pulpit, I kept wiping my face as if I were hot so no one would know that I was wiping away my tears. Finally, the deacons lowered the thermostat thinking that I was hot. Lowering the thermostat would not cool me off. It was hot, all right, but the atmosphere had nothing to do with it. There was a burning deep down in my soul challenging me to get it right.

As children of God, we are challenged to get it right. God depends upon us to get it right. Whatever God is calling us to do, He expects us to give it all that we've got. He expects us to put our hearts into it, and get it right. How are you doing? Can God depend upon you to get it right and continue in it?

105

"The Jews answered him, We have a law, and by our law he ought to die, because he made himself the Son of God." (John 19:7)

God does not do things just to be doing something. God has a purpose for everything that He does. God had a purpose for creating the world. Everything He created within the world has a purpose. God had a purpose for creating man and woman. God is a God of purpose and intentionality. God had a particular purpose for giving humankind laws. God established laws for us to follow because He loves us and has our best interest at heart. God gave us laws not to condemn us but to enable us to walk with Him and with one another. Without God-given laws, we humans would do what is right in our own sight. History has taught us that people become more like animals rather than people who were created in the image and likeness of God when that happens. It is never a good thing to ignore the laws of God. They are for our good. The laws of God should be our guiding principles in life.

There were times and are times when the very laws God has given to protect us and bring us closer to Him and to one another separate us from Him and from one another and are used to destroy the innocent. God-given laws in the hands of spiritually corrupt people can do more harm than good. This has always been the case. History is our witness. Many people who have confessed to being children of God have regularly taken God's Word and used it to enslave, dehumanize, torture, and kill those of another hue, even though they are also made in the image and likeness of God. Those same people who committed such atrocious crimes would go to church on Sunday; they would worship and praise God as if they had done God a favor by their appalling crime. I often wonder when God is going to answer the cry of those under the altar who have been slain and are crying out, "How long, O Lord?" (Revelation 6:10) These voices include all of those who have been abused and killed by those who ignore God's law and have no sense of value regarding human life.

As I reflect upon people using the God-given laws and His Word to abuse and destroy others, Jesus comes to mind. Those who were very religious and those who knew the law used the law to condemn the very one who gave them the law. They misused the law to condemn Jesus to death. Jesus' testimony regarding those that were crucifying Him was that they really did not know what they were doing. I am not sure that this statement of Jesus includes both the religious leaders and the Roman soldiers who implemented the crucifixion or just the Roman soldiers. But this I do know for sure: those who enslaved, dehumanized, tortured, and killed in the past knew precisely what they were doing. Those who ignore God's law today and deliberately abuse or kill others for whatever reason know exactly what they are doing. Are you misusing God's law to your evil design, or are you striving to allow His law to be your guide?

106

"In thee shall all families of the earth be blessed."
(Genesis 12:3b)

Like the man in the parable of the rich fool, so many go through life trying to gather all that they can. Those of us who know that all we have comes from the Lord appreciate God's blessings. We know for a fact that if the Lord chooses not to bless us, we will not be blessed. That is an undisputed fact. Knowing that our blessings come from the Lord God does not always help us to put things in the right perspective. Sometimes we seem to think that God has blessed us with so much just for ourselves. Some of us even tend to believe that God blesses us because somehow we believe we are worthy of such blessings. We think we have earned them; therefore, they are ours to do with as we please. Such thinking causes people to become very selfish and selective with their blessings. They only share with those who are able to share with them. They fail to become a real blessing to others which is a real disappointment to the Lord God.

We go through life thinking about ourselves and the few people who are connected to our world. We hardly ever think about those outside of our little world. We tend to believe that God has blessed us for ourselves. Keep in mind that I am referring to some who have made a profession of faith in Jesus Christ and attend His church regularly. On the other hand, many who claim to be agnostics have dedicated their lives to improving the lives of those who are not able to help themselves. They seem to understand more about how to use their accomplishments (blessings) than those of us who are always talking about how much we love Jesus. God has blessed us so that we can become a blessing to others. So often, rather than being a blessing to others we use God's blessings to separate us from others and look down on them. What a waste of God's resources.

All that we have belongs to God whether we acknowledge it or not. God has given some more and some less, but no matter what God has given us He expects us to be good stewards of His blessings. Whatever God has given us, He expects us to use some of it in such a way that we become a blessing to others. God blesses us so that we can bless others. That is the bottom line. Are you a blessing to others?

107

"So that I might finish my course with joy, and the ministry, which I have received of the Lord Jesus." (Acts 20:24)

I ran track one year when I was in high school. I ran the mile race. I knew that I would never win a race. It is not that I had no confidence in myself. I am just stating a fact. Even after many hours of serious training and giving my very best, I knew that I was not fast enough to win a race. I knew that I would not even come close to winning a race. The coach even knew that I was not going to win the race. I had no intention of winning the race even though I gave it my best. I knew for a fact that there would be many runners who were faster than I was. I guess by this time you are wondering why I would even enter such a race knowing that I had no chance of ever winning. The truth is that I did not enter the competition to win. The coach did not pick me because he thought I could win. The coach knew and I knew that I could finish the race. It would have been good if I could have won; however, my job was to finish the race. By completing the race, I would earn the team a point or two; therefore, I fulfilled my purpose for running in the race. My intention was not to win but to finish. In that light, I finished my course with joy.

So many people in life make the mistake of trying to be winners. They are very competitive. They are always trying to outdo others. They can't stand the idea of someone being better than they. They have to be number one, even at the expense of their family or a real friend. Many are taught to be the best from their youth. Such teaching at times causes them to embrace an aggressive attitude that causes them to make themselves the center of their lives. Life becomes all about them.

I have never embraced such an attitude. Such an attitude will cause one's focus to become out of focus. When that happens, people will focus on things that do not really matter. They will focus on things that have no lasting values. Instead of trying to be better than everyone else, I believe in being the best that I can be. God does not expect me to be better than everybody else. He expects me to be the best that I can be for His glory. Life has never been about winning. Winning is not a heavenly concept. It is a worldly concept. The heavenly concept regarding life is about finishing with joy. If we concentrate on finishing our course, God will give us some victories along the way.

What is your main concern in life? Is it about winning, or is it about finishing? When the apostle Paul came to the end of his earthly journey, he did not talk about being a winner. He spoke of being a finisher. He said, "I have fought a good fight, I have finished my course, I have kept the faith." (2 Timothy 4:7) It would be good if this is our testimony when we come to the end of our journey.

108

"Ye have compassed this mountain long enough:
turn you northward." (Deuteronomy 2:3)

There are times when we become too comfortable in our situation. When that happens, it is possible to lose sight of the big picture. In many instances, there is much more to life than what we are experiencing at the present moment. Too often, people tend to stay in their situation without any intention of moving on. Moving on in life takes courage and the willingness to take a risk. It is always easier to stay where we are than it is to move on. We are familiar with where we are. We know how to maneuver where we are. We know where to go and where not to go. We even feel to some degree that we are in control; therefore, it is much easier to stay where we are than it is to move on. Moving on is filled with too many uncertainties. Leaving that which is familiar to us is not always easy. We want to hold on to those things and people that are recognizable to us. Holding on to the familiar, at times, will cause people to miss out on blessings that are just beyond the horizon. There comes a time when we must recognize that we are not going anywhere because we have been doing the same thing over and over. It is time to move on.

We must keep in mind that the time to move on is not in our hands. It is a grave mistake to think that we are in complete control of our lives. There is one, (God), who holds the world in the palm of His hands. He not only holds the world in the palm of His hands, but He also holds us in the palm of His hands. God, and God alone, is in control of our lives whether we acknowledge it or not. God determines the when and the where. God will not make us move from our present

215

situation, but He will somehow let us know when to move and where to go because He loves us and has a plan for our lives. This plan of God's is always for our well-being. There is no doubt about that. God always has our best interest at heart. It behooves us to be obedient to the still small voice of God and move forward. "To day if ye will hear his voice, harden not your hearts, as in the provocation." (Hebrews 3:15) If we refuse to move at the beckoning of God's voice we will miss out on the particular blessings God has for us. To receive God's blessing, we must be where He wants us to be. We must never forget that God blesses us on His terms and not ours and that His blessings are never about merit. All of His blessings are impregnated with nothing but grace and mercy.

God informed the children of Israel that they had been traveling around the mountain for too long. It was time to turn northward. What about you? Have you been traveling in the same direction for too long? What is God saying about your journey? Is it time to turn northward?

109

*"Pleasant words **are as** an honeycomb, sweet to the soul,*
and health to the bones." (Proverbs 16:24)

Time and again, we go through each day without paying very much attention to our words. We say what we want to say when we want to say it and almost every time we want to say it. So many times, we fail to take the time to give serious consideration to the effect that our words have on others. There are times when we do not pay any attention to what we say. But on the other hand, more than a few people seriously consider every word that comes from our mouths. What we say matters to them. They have a great deal of respect for us. They believe in us. What we say will affect them in some way. It could affect them in a good way, or it could affect them in a bad way. There is enormous power in what we say. We can speak words that encourage people. We can also speak words that bring sorrow. Words are powerful. We can use them to tear down or to build up. Those of us who are wise choose our words carefully.

Through the years, children have been shaped by the words of their parents and peers. Many children grow up with low self-esteem because their parents and sometimes others had nothing good to say about them. Day in and day out, they were reminded that they could not do this or that, and they were never going to be worth anything. I remember turning in a class assignment one day, which was good. The teacher refused to accept my assignment and accused me of getting someone at home to do the assignment. She said, "You are not capable of doing such work; someone did this work for you." Then she paddled me and made me do the assignment again. After being devastated by the teacher I did the same assignment over, but this time the work was poorly done. The teacher looked at my work and said, "Now, this is what you are capable of doing." That teacher almost destroyed me. It took me many years to overcome her destructive words. With the help of God, I was finally able to overcome.

It would make all the difference in the world if every child grew up hearing encouraging and soothing words from their parents, teachers, and others in their neighborhood. It is no wonder that kind words are compared to a honeycomb. Honey not only tastes good but is very beneficial to one's health. Pleasant words are like honey in the sense that they add sweetness and fitness to a person's life. Words are impregnated with tremendous power. It would be very accommodating to speak words that have a positive influential implication and improve the lives of others. What about your words? Do they edify or do they dismantle?

110

"Arise, shine; for thy light is come, and the glory of the LORD is risen upon thee." (Isaiah 60:1)

The excellent news about frustrations, disappointments, pain, and despair is that these vicissitudes of life will pass. No storm in life will last forever. No matter how severe a storm is, God has a way of bringing us through. We can depend on God to do that. So, when the tide of life turns against us and we must swim upstream it would behoove us to concentrate on God rather than the tide. Focusing on the dangerous and challenging tide will cause us to complain and acquiesce. Thinking about God will inspire courage and hope. The Encarta Dictionary defined courage as "the ability to face danger, difficulty, uncertainty, or pain without being overcome by fear or being deflected from a chosen course of action." It is God's will that those who are called by His name will never be without courage, regardless of the trial. No matter what is going on God is in charge, and He always has our best interest at heart. "Biblical hope is the anticipation of a favorable outcome under God's guidance. More specifically, hope is the confidence that what God has done for us in the past guarantees our participation in what God will do in the future. Without courage and hope it would be complicated to make it through a storm.

Once God has brought us through the storm and we are walking in the sunshine, that is, our hopes and dreams are becoming a reality, we can thank God for bringing us through. Our adverse situation has changed because God has blessed us and is still blessing us. We no longer feel threatened by unfavorable circumstances we cannot control. God, and God alone, has smiled upon us, and we are walking in the light. It is time for us to "rise and shine, for thy light is come; and the glory of the LORD is risen upon thee." (Isaiah 60:1)

Now that we have been delivered, everyone that we come in contact with will know that the "glory of the LORD is risen upon us." They can tell by the way we carry ourselves. I remember years ago while I was working on a shopping center, a young man came up to me after working for about a month saying, "I was told that you are a preacher." I responded by confirming what he heard: "I am a preacher." He then said, "I had no idea that you were a preacher, but I knew for a fact that you are not one of us." The glory of the Lord had risen upon me, causing others to see something different about me. What about you? Has the glory of the Lord risen upon you, causing people to notice that you are different? It is that difference that attracts others to draw near to the Lord.

111

*"I was glad when they said unto me, Let us go
into the house of the LORD." (Psalm 122:1)*

There was a time, and it was not so long ago, that the Lord's house—the church—was the very center of the community. Everybody knew where the church was. If anyone came to town and wanted to know where a particular church was located, just about everybody could tell anyone where that particular church was. Most of the young people could tell you where a certain church was. Even those who did not go to church knew where the churches were located. The church was important.

That is not the case today. The church is no longer the center of the community. People feel that they can get along without the church. There are a few churches that are perpetually growing. Yes, there are a few mega-churches but for the most part there is a falling away from the church. People are leaving the church at an alarming rate, and race has nothing to do with it. They claim that the church is out of touch with reality. One person told me, "I don't see any reason to attend church any longer. It is not making a difference in my life. My life is the same, whether I go to church or not." Perhaps that is the reason that some "insiders" are becoming "outsiders," and "outsiders" are continuing to remain "outsiders."

A few years ago, I was in a particular community looking for a specific church. I saw a young man sitting on a porch. I stopped and asked him about this particular church location. He had no idea where this church was. When I did find the church, it was only one block from where the man was sitting on the porch. I assumed that the young man sitting on the porch did not attend the church that I had inquired about, or perhaps, he did not attend church at all. If that is true, it may be saying a lot about the young man concerning what he thinks about the church. On the other hand, it could be saying a lot about the church regarding what the church thinks about the young man. It seems that the young man was out of touch with the church, and the church was out of touch with the young man. Perhaps the young man was not seeking the church, and maybe the church was not seeking the young man. The young man was in a spiritually dark place because he had surmised that he did not need the church. He had concluded that the church had nothing to offer him. It seems as if the church was in a spiritually dark place, because she had reneged on her commitment to Jesus to go into the hedges and highways and compel men and women to come to Jesus.

Perhaps it is because the church is in a spiritually dark place that those in the church are not excited about going to church. They cannot declare with the psalmist, "I was glad when they said unto me, Let us go into the house of the LORD." (Psalm 122:1) If we are not excited about attending church, should we think that those we invite should be excited about visiting our church? You know the answer to that question. People want to be a part of something alive and vibrant. People want to be a part of something that is innovating and encouraging. When we are permeated with gladness about attending our place of worship, others will come to see why we are excited. The spirit of gladness is contagious. Are you excited about attending your church?

112

"I am debtor both to the Greeks, and to the Barbarians;
both to the wise, and to the unwise. So, as much as in me is,
I am ready to preach the gospel to you that are at Rome also."
(Romans 1:14–15)

Many books have been written about debt-free living. The truth is that thousands upon thousands have no desire to be out of debt. They enjoy being in debt because being in debt makes them look good. It makes them feel as if they have arrived. When people see their new cars, beautiful house, and fancy clothes, it makes them feel like somebody. It is a fact that most people like to feel like somebody. The problem is that too many people are seeking self-worth in all the wrong places. They are seeking self-worth in material things which leads to self-imposed and self-perpetuated debt that keeps them in bondage. People are in debt because of their poor choices, impulse purchases, and attempts to keep up with the Jones. They remain in bondage due to high-interest rates and low minimum payments. People of all races are swiftly accelerating toward an abysmal future in which it is almost impossible to overcome their financial cavity.

Becoming debt-free is a worthy goal to work toward. Unnecessary debt can cause one to live a life of misery. Many are overworked, tired, and on the verge of a nervous breakdown. Families are being torn apart because of redundant debt. People are suffering spiritually because of preventable debt. Some debts are reasonable and necessary. Such debts make life pleasant and comfortable. Some debts are reasonable and necessary while others are ridiculous and unnecessary.

As it relates to being in debt the words, "I am debtor both to the Greeks, and to the Barbarians; both to the wise, and to the unwise," are extraordinarily poignant and captivating. This reminds me of a debt that we should take to our grave. It is a sin with devastating consequences to allow this debt to be delinquent. The world is in the shape it is in today because this debt is being neglected. Too many feel as if they have no obligation to other human beings. That is simply not the truth. If you are alive on this earth you cannot truthfully say that you owe no one. Every human being is his brother's keeper. There is no way around that. We are all obligated to every human being with no strings attached. We are obligated for both their spiritual and physical well-being. There is no doubt about it; only death releases us from this particular debt. How are you doing concerning this debt? The world would be better off if you pay this debt—the debt of being your brother's keeper.

113

*"By this shall all men know that ye are my disciples, if ye have love
one to another. A new commandment I give unto you, That ye love
one another; as I have loved you, that ye also love one another."*
(John 13:34, 35)

A certain man of significant influence questioned Jesus one day about
the greatest commandment. Jesus responded by saying, "The first
of all the commandments *is*, Hear, O Israel; The Lord our God is one
Lord: And thou shalt love the Lord thy God with all thy heart, and
with all thy soul, and with all thy mind, and with all thy strength: this
is the first commandment. And the second *is* like, *namely* this, Thou
shalt love thy neighbour as thyself. There is none other commandment
greater than these." (Mark 12:29-31) The two greatest commandments
are rooted and grounded in love for God and love for humankind. As
it relates to our love for God, we must love Him with our whole being;
therefore, nothing can interfere or take the place of the love we have
for God. It is the same way with God. God is love, and since He is love,
He allows nothing to separate us from His love. As it relates to our
love for our neighbor, which refers to fellow human beings in general,
we should love other human beings as we love ourselves. The love we
have for ourselves should be directed toward others. Such love should
always look out for the best interest of oneself and the best interest of
others. These two commandments of love should govern our thoughts,
decisions, and actions. When we come to those crossroads in life, and
we are not sure which way to go, we should ask ourselves which way
will display love for God and love for others.

The apostle John tells us, "We know that we have passed from death unto life, because we love the brethren." (1 John 3:14) Again, the emphasis is on love for others. This love guarantees us that we have a home with God in eternity. Love is of extreme importance in the Christian's life. Love is the nature of the Christian life. Without love, it is impossible to prove that we belong to Him. Loving others does not earn us a place in eternity with God, but it does prove that we have a mansion in eternity.

Jesus tells His disciples, "A new commandment I give unto you, That ye love one another; as I have loved you, that ye also love one another. By this shall all men know that ye are my disciples, if ye have love one to another." (John 13:34, 35) Once again, the love for others is highlighted. We are called to love others based on Jesus' sacrificial love for us. Jesus expressed God's love everywhere He went. We are to do likewise. This love is the proof of discipleship. It is impossible to elude love and remain a true disciple of Jesus. That is very frightening, isn't it? We tend to love those who are like us. We even love a few of those who are different from us. This world is lacking in love especially among those who call themselves Christians. Something is seriously wrong with this picture. When are we going to get it right?

114

*"Then David the king stood up upon his feet, and said, Hear me, my brethren, and my people: **As for me**, I **had** in mine heart to build an house of rest for the ark of the covenant of the LORD, and for the footstool of our God, and had made ready for the building: But God said unto me, Thou shalt not build an house for my name, because thou **hast been** a man of war, and hast shed blood."*
(1 Chronicles 28:2, 3)

Every good intention is not of the Lord. That may seem strange to you. You are convinced that every good idea or plan comes directly from the Lord. You may be one of many who get ideas from others. These ideas worked well in a certain place and because of that you think they will work where you are. That is not always the case. That plan was for that particular place or that particular person. It is not for you or your organization or church. Specific plans only work in certain places. Perhaps your plan was original, that is, you thought of it yourself. You carefully examined the plan and decided that it was a good plan. It was a workable plan, and it would benefit many. You were excited about your plan, and you could not wait to introduce your plan and put it into action. You even talked to God about your plan. You spoke to Him about how good your plan is and how beneficial it would be. You even asked Him to help you put this plan into action and bless your plan. The problem is that you never once thought about whether your plan, even though it was good, was in sync with God's plan. Every good plan is not necessarily God's plan, and that is a fact. We need to stop taking that for granted.

Throughout the years this has been a serious problem for people, especially God's people. People all over the world are living unfulfilled lives because their lives are completely out of sync with God's plan for their lives. In the eyes of the world, they are successful and a great role model. They have everything that is associated with success from a worldly point of view. In the light of all their success, honors, and awards many of them are not happy and are on the verge of an emotional breakdown. They are living a successful life and an unfulfilled life at the same time. That is the real recipe for disappointment and disaster.

Real success is not about fame and fortune; it is about living out God's plan for your life. That could simply mean that you just might be a failure in the eyes of the world, but in the eyes of God your story is a different story. It is different and a real success story because somewhere along the way you discovered your plan was not God's plan for your life. Your plan and God's plan were two different plans, even though your plan was good. Perhaps you were shaken and confused at first but, finally, you acquiesced.

David had a good plan. He planned to build God a house. Many would have commended David for having such a good plan. The problem with David's plan is that it was not God's plan even though it was an excellent plan. The good news is that David discovered that his plan was not God's plan; therefore, he surrendered to God's plan. The question is whose plan are you following? Are you following your plan, someone else's plan, no plan at all, or God's plan?

115

"Therefore, my beloved brethren, be ye stedfast, unmoveable,
always abounding in the work of the Lord, forasmuch as ye know
that your labour is not in vain in the Lord."
(1 Corinthians 15:58)

The world is more of a battleground than a playground. As children of God, we are placed on a battlefield. We don't have a choice in this matter if we are who we say we are. By our very nature, we were born to fight the good fight. Fighting is what soldiers are trained to do. The warfare we are engaged in is not "against flesh and blood, but against principalities, against powers, against the rulers of the darkness of this world, against spiritual wickedness in high places." (Ephesians 6:12) Amid such great and devastating enemies, we are to verify the predominance of life over death, declare the gospel of Jesus Christ, and to live as if we know Him. We are called to stay focused as we journey through a world that is entirely out of focus.

Not only must we stay focused, but we must also challenge the world to change its focus from a world-oriented focus to a heavenly oriented focus. This can be dangerous. It could cost us very much. As soldiers, we are willing to pay the cost. We know that our end is far greater than our beginning. Our beginning started as we embraced Jesus Christ as Savior, along with all of His promises. He promised us that we shall live again in a prepared place with Him in eternity, and that we will look like Him. It is these promises along with others that motivate us to take hold of our responsibilities as soldiers of the cross.

We know that time is winding down, and that we don't have any time to waste. We are commanded to redeem the time and not waste time. Wasted time cannot be recalled. It is gone forever. We have much work to do for the kingdom. God depends upon us. We cannot afford to live for our glory. We must not be about our own business. We must be about God's business, and invite others to join us in kingdom work. The work that we do for the Lord will not be in vain. The Lord God will make sure of that. When it is all said and done, we will be rewarded for our work; therefore, it would behoove us to "be ye stedfast, unmoveable, always abounding in the work of the Lord, forasmuch as ye know that your labour is not in vain in the Lord." What about you? Are you going to let difficult people dissuade you from engaging in kingdom work, or are you going to be faithful unto the end?

116

*"I hate **vain** thoughts: but thy law do I love."*
(Psalm 119:113)

The word love is one of the most misused words in the entire world. We say that we love everybody because it is our Christian duty to do so, but at the same time we act like we don't love anybody. Love always has the best interest of the other person at heart. In other words, if we love someone, we will strive to do the right thing concerning them at all times. Love always does the right thing or at least attempts to do the right thing. Love is much more than talk. It is much more than an emotional feeling about someone or something. Love can be used as a noun. Love is one of the greatest needs of this world. That is the truth. But to use the word love as a noun and never as a verb will always leave the world starving for real love. The word love is much more effective when it is used as a verb. When used as a verb love begins to embrace certain kind actions to express it. Such action is always unselfish, sacrificial, and endless. Love is much more than talk. Love is something that we do and that something is the right thing. If we love someone, we will never intentionally do anything to hurt them. We will not steal from them. In every situation we will do the loving thing. The loving thing is always in sync with God's Word.

We should always examine our lives to make sure that what we do for others is out of pure love. Those of us who are called by His name are driven by love because we have experienced the love of God. We are always conscious of the fact that "God so loved the world, that he gave his only begotten Son, that whosoever believeth in him should

231

not perish, but have everlasting life," (John 3:16) It is this wonderful love of God that compels us to love Him and others.

Since we love God, we love what He loves and dislike what He dislikes. Therefore, like the psalmist, we dislike half-hearted devotion to the Lord God. We love God, and we love God's Word. The love that we have for God's Word constrains us to strive to be wholly devoted to His Word. When we think of just how much God loves us we are driven to dislike all unfaithfulness to His Word. What about you? Are you faithfully endeavoring to keep God's Word?

117

"And it shall come to pass, that before they call, I will answer;
and while they are yet speaking, I will hear."
(Isaiah 65:24)

Prayer is communication with God. This suggests at least two things. We talk to God, and God listens to us. It also means that God talks to us, and we listen to Him. It is impossible to separate prayer from the lives of those who have established a personal relationship with God the Father through God the Son. Perhaps we don't always pray as we should pray, but we always strive to pray. The Bible teaches us to pray and faint not. This suggests that if we fail to pray, we are not going to make it. In that light, we make every attempt to make prayer a very part of our being. Vance Havner was right when he said, "Our Lord found both time ('a great while before day') and place ('a solitary place') for prayer. We are hard put to it these days to find either, but find them we must, for what we are at prayer is what we are and nothing more."

There are times when it is downright difficult to pray. There are several reasons for this. Sometimes, we are too distracted to pray. Like Martha, we are distracted by much service. When we think of the many prayers that were not answered according to our desire, we sometimes fail to pray. There are moments when we surmise that God is going to do what He wants to do anyway, so what is the use of praying about it. Then there are times when our prayers are so repetitious that we become discouraged, and we fail to pray as we should. There are also moments when we are completely out of fellowship with God, and we fail to pray. All of these reasons and other reasons are weapons that the devil uses to keep us from praying as we should. The only way to be victorious over the devil in the area of prayer is that we must watch and pray.

The prophet talks about a time when the people of God will experience total blessedness. Disaster and misfortune will be a thing of the past. God will bless every generation. On that day, God will hear and answer the prayers of His people before they pray. What a difference it would make today if God's people everywhere would take time to pray. The Lord God would replace the gods of our own making. He would become the center of our lives. There would be no limit to God's blessings if only people would turn to God in prayer. Prayer will help usher in God's kingdom. Paradise will be restored. There will be no more violence, no more racism, no more injustice.

What are you waiting for to turn to the Lord in prayer? "And it shall come to pass, that before they call, I will answer; and while they are yet speaking, I will hear. The wolf and the lamb feed together, and the lion shall eat straw like the bullock; and dust shall be the serpent's meat. They shall not hurt nor destroy in all my holy mountain, saith the Lord." (Isaiah 65:24–25)

118

"Lo children are an heritage of the Lord."
(Psalm 127:3a)

For many children one of the most beautiful and poignant senses in the entire Bible is that of Jesus taking a child and putting him by His side. Jesus did this to teach His disciples a lesson on true greatness, a lesson that is very important to those who are in leadership. However, for many children the lesson is not about Jesus teaching about greatness but a lesson on love. Jesus loves little children. That is the most wonderful lesson of all. God loves us and cares about us, and we are special in His sight.

Knowing that God loves us makes us feel a sense of worth. Even though we did not know very much about God or His Word, we knew that God loved us. Knowing that God loved us also made us feel good. We were unique in His sight. That mattered to us as little children.

Just as God loves little children, we should also love little children. Children are precious gifts from God. Parents must confess that each child is a gift from God, an expression of divine favor. Children are a blessing from God and not a burden. They are a manifestation of God's goodness upon one's life, and they bring great pleasure to the home. They have a way of making a home complete.

Although children are a blessing and a gift from God, they seem to be less appreciated these days. Many parents refrain from having children because they are seen as a burden rather than a blessing. Children today are so rebellious that some adults have decided that it is better not to have them. It takes time, strength, money, love, and sacrifices to rear children and to see them go against everything they have been taught is not worth it. The society in which we live is so corrupt, tempting, and dangerous that it is almost impossible for children to avoid the terrible pitfalls set for them. As a result, some have decided that they would be better off without children.

Such ideology is contrary to the Bible. The Bible teaches us to be fruitful and multiply and that children are a heritage to the Lord. Suppose the parents of Charles Richard Drew—the physician responsible for America's first significant blood bank—decided that the world was too sinful to bring a child into the world. Suppose the parents of Marie Van Brittan Brown, who along with her husband developed a way for a motorized camera to peer through a set of peepholes and project images onto a TV monitor, decided not to have a child because it would be impossible for her to avoid the terrible pitfalls set for her. Suppose the parents of Barack Obama had reasoned it was not in their best interest to have a child.

Children are God's gift to the world. We are to cherish and raise them in a way that is pleasing to the Lord. Many children have grown up and made a great contribution to the world. The world would never be the same without them. Perhaps you will never be one who will make a contribution that will change the world. Despite that, it is possible for you to be the person that will change a child's life and that child just might do something positive to change the world. Are you willing to embrace and encourage the little children who are part of your little world, regardless of who they are and how they look?

119

"Thus speaketh the LORD of hosts, saying, This people say, The time is not come, the time that the LORD'S house should be built."
(Haggai 1:2)

Too many people hide behind excuses. Rather than implementing that which they know they ought to do, they make excuses for not doing it. They seem to be completely satisfied with excuses. Allowing their responsibilities to go undone is no problem for them. Their excuses seem to outweigh their responsibility. Their excuses seem to be more important than their accountability. An excuse is a reason which people use to explain why something has not been done. It is easier to make up some kind of excuse for not doing something than it is to get involved and do something. Too many dreams have gone unfilled because of excuses. Too many children have fallen by the wayside because parents have come up with excuses to avoid rearing them as they should. Too many children have missed out on a good solid education because they had too many excuses to keep them from studying. Real kingdom work is taking place on a small scale because God's people have too many excuses for not getting involved in kingdom work. Too much time has been wasted; too many opportunities have been lost; too many lives have been shattered; too many lives have gone astray; too many talents have been misplaced and misused; and too many people are not engaged in kingdom work because they can always come up with what they think is a genuine excuse not to do so. No matter how important a thing is, there seems to be a more important excuse or excuses to keep one from doing that important thing. This world is full of excuses. There seem to be more excuses for not doing the right and significant things than there are reasons for doing them.

People have become so obsessed with their own lives that they have little time for the thing that matters in life, which is kingdom work. We know in theory that life is about God and not about us. When it comes to practice, that is an altogether different thing; it is all about us. We are so busy thinking about ourselves and looking good in the eyes of others that we do not have much time for God and His work, much less the time to love our neighbor as we love ourselves and to be our brother's keeper. We don't have time to do these things.

So it was in the days of Haggai. The people were so busy doing their own thing that they did not have time for the things of God, especially building the Lord's house which was a place of worship. They had grown apathetic to the worship of God. When challenged by Haggai to rebuild the temple, they said, "The time has not come." In other words, they were saying, "We have more important things to do." What about you? When you are challenged to commit yourself to kingdom work, how do you respond? Do you accept the challenge, or do you come up with an excuse?

ACKNOWLEDGMENTS

First and foremost, I would like to thank the Lord God for inspiring me to write this book. Without Him this book would not exist, for it is in Him and Him alone that I live and am able to move about and accomplish certain things.

This may sound strange to some, but I would also like to thank my loving wife, Nella, who made her transition to be with the Lord after thirty-eight years of marriage. There are times when I can still feel her presence encouraging me to run this race with endurance, always leaning and depending on Jesus, our Lord and Savior. I thank God for my adult children, and I would like to thank them for their encouragement along the way.

Thanks to Royce Brown and Dr. Melvia Russell for reading and rereading the manuscript, making corrections and giving me feedback. They read the manuscript as if it were their own. Thanks to Rev. Trevor Crenshaw, Rev. Keith Shoulders, and Rev. Daylon Woodall. Their support and encouragement have been incredible.

Made in the USA
Columbia, SC
23 September 2023

23300651R00134